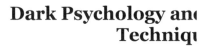 **Dark Psychology and Techniqu**

A Useful Guide to Learn How to Improve your Mind skills and empathy.

By
Jason Wolf

Introduction

Dark Psychology is manipulative art and science, as well as control of the mind. While Psychology is basically the study of human behavior and is central to our actions, interactions, and thoughts, the concept of Dark Psychology is the phenomena through which people use tactics of persuasion, motivation, coercion, and manipulation to get what they actually want.

Narcissism-Grandiosity, lack of empathy, and Selfishness.

Psychopathy – Sometimes attractive and polite and marked by impulsiveness, loss of empathy, selfishness, and guilt.

None of us like to be the object of manipulation, however very frequently it occurs. We might not be exposed to anyone directly in the Dark Triad but on a regular basis, we experience dark psychology strategies with average, ordinary people like you and me.

These strategies are mostly found in commercials, sales techniques, web ads, and even the behaviors of our manager. If you have children (especially teenagers) you would most likely witness such strategies when your kids play with behaviors to obtain what they want and try control for themselves. In fact, the people you trust and love often use dark persuasion and covert manipulation. Here are some of the tactics that an ordinary, everyday people use most often.

Machiavellianism – Use of manipulation to exploit and deceive people, and has no moral sense.

Love Flooding-Compliments, buttering someone or affection

Love Rejection-Withstand devotion and affection

Lying-Amplification, falsehoods, incomplete truths, fake tales

Withdrawal-Avoiding the person or treatment in silence

Restriction of choice – Giving certain options that distract you from the choice you don't want someone to make actually

Semantic manipulation – Using those words that are supposed to have a mutual or common definition, but later the manipulator tells you that he or she has a different definition of the conversation and understanding. Words are strong and they allow imports.

While some people who use dark tactics know exactly what they do and are willing to manipulate you to get what they want, others are using dark and inhumane tactics without being completely aware of it. All of these individuals learned techniques from their parents throughout their youth. Others learned the techniques by happenstance in their adulthood or teenage years. They unintentionally used a manipulative tactic and it worked. They did have what they wanted. And they keep using strategies to help them get their way.

People are trained in some cases to use those tactics. Typically your sales or marketing programs or sales are training programs that instruct unethical psychological, dark, and persuasion tactics. Many of these schemes use dark techniques to create a logo or sell a product solely for the purpose of getting serve themselves or their business, not the client. Many of the training programs persuade people that the use of such tactics is fine and is in the buyer's interest. Because, naturally, when they buy the product or service, their lives will get much better.

Who is using Dark Psychology and the tactics of manipulation? Here's a list of those people who seem to make the most of those tactics.

Reverse Psychology – Say one thing to a person or perform it with the aim of inspiring them to do the contrary that is actually what you want.

Narcissists – Really narcissistic people (meeting the clinical diagnosis) usually have an exaggerated sense of self-worth. They also need others to affirm their conviction that they are superior. They've dreamed of being adored and worshipped. To preserve them, they use techniques of dark ideology, coercion, and dishonest intimidation.

Sociopaths – People that are genuinely sociopathic (meeting the clinical diagnosis), are frequently intelligent, charming, yet impulsive. They use dark propagandas to build up a relationship that is superficial and further take advantage of people because of a lack of emotionality as well as the ability to feel remorse.

Attorneys – A few attorneys aim to win their case so intently that they resort to using dark manipulation strategies to have the result they want to get.

Selfish people – Whoever has a self-agenda before others can be this. First, they will use strategies to satisfy their own needs, even at the cost of someone else. They don't mind win-losing results.

Politicians – Some of the politicians use these dark psychological techniques and dark tactics of persuasion to persuade people that they are right, and to get votes even.

Salespeople – Almost all salespeople get so focused on getting a sale that they use these dark techniques to encourage and persuade somebody to buy their stuff.

Leaders-Few of the leaders uses dark tactics from their subordinates to obtain greater effort, compliance, or higher performance.

Public Speakers – A few speakers also use these dark tactics to enhance the audience's emotional state of knowing it leads to more products being sold at the back of the scene.

MANIPULATION TECHNIQUES

Most individuals indulge in regular exploitation. For example, telling someone you feel "okay" when you are genuinely depressed is technically a type of manipulation because it regulates the responses and attitudes of your acquaintance towards you.

Nevertheless, coercion may often have more subtle effects and is sometimes related to emotional violence, particularly in interpersonal relationships. Most people perceive coercion negatively, particularly when it affects the exploited person's physical, social, or mental wellbeing.

Although individuals who exploit others sometimes do so because they feel the need to dominate their behavior and climate, an instinct sometimes arising from deep-seated insecurity or anxiety, it is not safe behavior. Engaging in manipulation will keep the manipulator from communicating with their own selves, so being deceived will contribute to a broad variety of adverse effects being encountered.

Chapter 1: What Is Manipulation?

The purpose of manipulation is to use manipulative methods to regulate attitudes, feelings, and relationships. Manipulation in certain instances tends to be so strong that it leads a person to doubt their view of truth. One such tale demonstrated in the iconic film Gaslight, in which a woman's husband secretly deceived her until she no longer respected her own beliefs. For example, the husband clandestinely shut the gaslights off and persuaded his wife that the darkening light was all in her mind.

9.1 Manipulation's Impact on Emotional Wellbeing

Manipulation, if left unresolved, can result in negative mental health outcomes for all those manipulated. Chronic coercion in intimate relationships can also be an indication of emotional violence that may, in certain situations, have a similar impact as trauma — especially where the person is made to feel bad or embarrassed.

Victims of persistent manipulation may:

• Feel depressed

• Rising fear

• Build inappropriate management habits

• Seek to appease this dishonest guy continuously

• Lie regarding emotions

• Put the interests of another human before themselves

• Having trouble believing people

Mental well-being and Manipulation

Although most people occasionally take part in manipulation, a severe form of manipulation may indicate a more serious concern for mental health.

Manipulation is more common in the diagnosis of a personality disorder like emotionally more unstable personality (BPD) and narcissistic personality (NPD). Manipulation can be a medium for many with BPD to meet their emotional needs or get validation and often happens when the person with BPD feels insecure or deserted. As several individuals with BPD have encountered or endured violence, coercion may have evolved implicitly as a tool for dealing with their needs.

Individuals with a negative personality (NPD) can have different explanations for coercive behavior. Because those with NPD may fail to establish intimate partnerships, they may turn to coercion to "win" their spouse in the partnership. Features of manipulative abuse can involve bullying, accusing, playing the "victim," problems of dominance, and gaslighting.

Munchausen syndrome due to Proxy, through which a caregiver turns another adult to become sick for sympathy or love, is another disorder marked by deceptive behavior.

1.2 Relationship Manipulation

Long-term manipulation, such as those between friends, family members, and romantic partners, can have severe effects in close relations. Manipulation may weaken a relationship's wellbeing and contribute to the poor mental stability of those in the partnership or even relationship breakdown.

Manipulation may lead one person in a marriage or relationship to feel threatened, lonely, or useless. Also in stable partnerships, one spouse can exploit the other unintentionally to prevent conflict, or just to try and protect their spouse from feeling burdened. Some individuals might already realize that their friendship is being exploited, and prefer to ignore it or downplay it. Manipulation in romantic relationships can take multiple shapes, such as exaggeration, remorse, gift-giving, or the selective display of affection, secrecy, and passive aggression.

Adults who manipulate their kids can set up their kids for shame, depression, anxiety, eating disorders, and other psychological problems. One research has shown that parents who use coercion techniques on their kids may actually raise the risk that their kids may use coercive actions. Signs of coercion in the partnership between parent and child that include having the child feel bad, a parent's lack of responsibility, downplaying the successes of a child, and a desire to be active in certain facets of the child's existence.

People may even feel exploited when they're part of a dysfunctional relationship. One individual can use the other in deceptive partnerships to satisfy their own needs, at the cost of their friend's. A dishonest friend might use remorse or manipulation to gain things such as issuing loans, or they may approach the person only when they need to fulfill their own emotional needs, and may make excuses when their friend needs help.

Examples of Manipulative Conduct

Often, individuals can unintentionally influence others without becoming completely informed of what they are doing, whilst others can deliberately seek to improve their coercion techniques. Several indications of manipulation are:

• Passive- Violent Actions

• Associated threats

• Injustice

• Withholding facts

• A person alienated from loved ones

• Gas-lighting

• Taking advantage of gender to achieve goals

• Verbal abuse

Given that the intentions behind manipulation can fluctuate from unconscious to deceitful, it is vital to recognize the manipulative circumstances that are taking place. While breaking it down can be crucial in harassment cases, a psychiatrist can help you learn to cope with or tackle certain people's abusive behaviors.

1.3 How to Treat Misleading People

If manipulation is harmful it may be difficult to cope with certain people's behavior. Workplace manipulation has been shown to decrease performance, and loved ones' manipulative actions can make reality appear questionable. If you feel exploited in some kind of partnership, it may be beneficial to:

• Shutdown. When someone wants to get out of you a specific emotional reaction, prefer not to hand them one. For example, if you are known to impress a manipulative buddy before asking for an overstepping favor, don't play along — rather, respond kindly and change the discussion.

• Show confidence. Manipulation may also involve attempts by one individual to allow another to question their ability, instincts, or even truth. When this occurs, keeping to the narrative will help; but, if this happens regularly in a tight relationship, it may be time to quit.

• Stay on topic. If you point out conduct that leaves you feeling manipulated, the other individual may attempt to limit the situation, or muddle the scenario by bringing other issues. Remember and stick to your point of principle.

• Handle the issue. Point out the deceptive conduct as it happens. Maintaining a focus on how bad the behavior of the other individual affects you instead of beginning with a judgmental statement may also help you come to a resolution while stressing that their manipulative strategies won't work on you.

Tackling Therapy Manipulation

Treatment and counseling for manipulative behavior may greatly depend on what underlying problems are resulting in the issue. For example, if the manipulation is a result of an underlying mental health problem, personal therapy could help that person realize why their conduct is unhealthy to themselves and others around them. A therapist may also be able to assist the manipulative individual to learn skills to interact with others while honoring their limits and addressing underlying emotions that may contribute to the behavior.

Some mental health problems, such as borderline personality, can trigger people to feel insecure about relationships, causing them to behave manipulatively to feel healthy. In these situations, a therapist can help the individual overcome their mental health problem, which may in effect minimize their distress and make them feel comfortable in their partnerships.

Chapter 2: Covert Emotional Manipulation

Several of the dark psychology tactics that you'll find use this type of emotional manipulation in one way or another. You will recognize signs of CEM as you learn more about the world of dark psychology, and it's various forms. And knowing precisely what CEM consists of is a crucial first phase towards recognizing the nature of manipulation. Covert emotional manipulation is one person's way to manipulate another's thoughts and feelings in an underhand manner which is undetected by the manipulated person.

2.1 Concept of Covert Emotional Manipulation

Breaking down each of the three terms in the title is a perfect

way to get a grip on the simple concept. Covert refers to the way in which certain manipulators can conceal their intentions and the true nature of their actions. It is not possible to categorize any emotional exploitation and power as hidden. However, targets of the hidden sort usually do not realize they have been exploited, do not recognize how coercion has been done, and may not even be able to infer the motive of their manipulator. CEM is a dark Stealth psychology bomber, avoiding detection and defense until too late. The mental aspect of treating relates to the manipulator's personal emphasis. Other possible forms of manipulation require the attitudes, values, and motivation of the individuals. Focuses on CEM Specifically influencing the mental condition and perception of an individual.

This area of influence is the focus of manipulators as they know that an individual's emotions are central to all other facets of his or her personality. Manipulating the feelings of others is like breaking their jugular vein. In case a Person has emotional control, they have control over their feelings. The final piece of this mystery is the word "coercion." power and manipulation are similar things is a widespread misconception. This isn't the case. Manipulation refers to the dirty tricks and hidden process of influence occurring outside of the consciousness of the person being regulated. Another big distinction is the purpose behind influencing somebody else, as opposed to the intent behind manipulating them. An influencing person has the mindset of "I want to support you make choices that are beneficial for you." A manipulator has the mindset of "I want to subtly manipulate you to favor me." Therefore, knowing the purpose of any action is simply a question of determining whether or not it is an indication of hidden emotional exploitation. Now you've had an explanation of just what is hidden emotional coercion and whether it's distinct from other types of control. I will now explore the most likely situations to find arising covert emotional manipulation, as well as the major types of manipulative characters that occur time after time again.

2.2 Manipulators in Different Situations

Broadly speaking, there are four main situations where indirect exploitation of emotions may occur. Professional, personal, romantic, and family. By far the most common situation is romantic covert emotional manipulation, and can also be the most fatal. However, less apparent forms of CEM can be seen almost everywhere. Once you know the idea and its practical applications, you'll be able to defend against it, regardless of the circumstances you're in. Just as there are popular scenarios where covert emotional manipulation can take place, there are prevalent kinds of people who develop the ideas that underlie CEM. Being able to link the CEM theory to real, individual portrayals of its concepts is an important element of fully understanding it. A dictating life partner is a frequently noted illustration of CEM principles. When someone is in a marriage, and their husband is clearly attempting to control them, the individual is expected to be disgusted with what's going on and is looking to find some way out of that. Because of this, many regulating partners exert their effects in the most secretive way possible. Their girlfriend or wife tends to end up becoming a target of utter sexual abuse, without even knowing that it is happening. This gives the manipulator the power they want without any threat of being detected and having lost the other person for better. Also, a so-called "buddy" could use CEM to get the result they want out of their connection with someone else. One of the more popular forms of manipulators in this specific category is someone who deliberately triggers in a person the emotions of remorse, compassion, and responsibility toward them. The person manipulated in this way will not be aware they are being affected. They won't be able to demonstrate why they feel and act toward their "friend," the manipulator, the way they do. Further prevalent play area for covert emotional tricksters is the professional field. Numerous people have tales about working for a supervisor, or some powerful figure, that appeared to cause unexplained feelings about remorse, anxiety, or obligation in them. People who have been exploited in this way have never been able to identify why those emotions exist and where they originate. Within the CEM world, family situations are among the most troubling. A skillful manipulator who can locate a victim within his or her own family is probable to be very harmful in terms of their influence. That is because CEM is an effective tactic particularly though the manipulator and target do not have a truly strong relation to one another. The degree of power and leverage will rise dramatically when the true bond of the blood link is applied to the mix. Why are familial situations so suitable for using CEM? To put it plainly, people are now experiencing a sense of moral responsibility to support people out of their own families to "go the extra mile" and ensure that their needs are met. The hidden emotional manipulation activities contribute to the current predisposition to control, and the effect is a rather soft target. So how precisely do clandestine mental manipulators continue to instill the power of their victims at these levels? They have a variety of techniques that are challenging to spot, yet much more difficult to avoid.

2.3 Methods

You already understand the concept of covert emotional manipulation and the types of circumstances in which it will happen. This is a strong general overview of the topic, but it is also necessary to consider some of the different techniques that manipulators use to gain power. This form of emotional abuse has the entire function of having it as untraceable as possible. This segment is aimed at blowing this underground universe wide open for all to recognize.

Love bombing

Love bombing is a tactic commonly used by relational manipulators at the outset of their relationship with a target. It includes the serious, unexpected, and aggressive show of good feelings towards a victim. Which can at first appear counterintuitive. If someone wants to injure others, why do they immediately behave so intensively positive? Because it has its own purposes! The idea behind love bombing is that it generates an overwhelming feeling of confidence, intimacy, and loyalty towards the manipulator from a victim. The severity to which love bombing is used, and the individuals from whom it is used, depends on the situation assessment by the manipulator. A target who is alone, depressed, and needing help and consolation will definitely be more deeply and freely bombarded with affection because the manipulator thinks they will be responsive to it. Likewise, a more rooted target would need a less severe and subtler positivity assault. One can learn two valuable lessons about CEM from the description of the technique of love bombing. First of all, it beautifully demonstrates the hidden existence of CEM. Imagine trying to understand the bombardment of love as something bad. "Okay, this guy was really sweet to me and made me feel pretty happy." It's doubtful that such a comment would cause any alarm bells or warning signs of violence. This is a textbook example of how anything that has a bad impact may be interpreted as optimistic. The second clear message we should gain from knowing love bombing about CEM is how CEM is tailored to the particular circumstance that each target poses. Experienced manipulators in their history would have secretly manipulated other men, and evolved through the encounter. Therefore in any particular scenario, they know the best strength and pacing of any specific CEM technique. For example, every person responds to different "loving" gestures differently. Compliments function well on some, while gifts affect others more than others. If someone who has not been trained in the CEM sector has attempted to love a target, it is doubtful that they would have a lot of success.

This is because it requires knowledge of the exact extent to which a victim reacts to certain methods and not to others. Just as a Dr. can recommend the right dose, so the dark manipulator can use the correct amount of manipulation.

Reinforcement

Intermittent constructive reinforcement is a commonly practiced procedure that follows love bombing. It is a means of controlling a victim without them realizing what is happening to them. The standard sequence of a CEM scenario in the textbook includes love bombing accompanied by optimistic Strengthening and intermittent positive attention. The justification for this sequence is now being clarified. Love bombing in the early days of their relationship is the pure, unearned, and extreme show of optimism from a manipulator to their target. It is meant to weaken the defenses of a survivor, enhance their dependence on the individual who manipulates them, and establish the context of a supportive partnership, intimacy, or whatever other shapes the contact takes. After love-bombing the next move is always constructive affirmation. That is a conduct reversal, through which the manipulator no longer displays unending, pure positivity towards their target.

Instead, the manipulator withholds some sort of positivity until a period when the target demonstrates a desirable action. So, for instance, if the manipulator wants their victim to regularly call them, the manipulator will only exhibit a better answer when that happens. The target may be uncertain of the strategic manipulation with positive feedback toward them but will subconsciously agree with the manipulator's desire to enjoy the pleasant feelings on display. This positive strengthening is then substituted by intermittent positive strengthening or IPR. IPR requires avoiding positivity gestures, even though a positive activity is seen.

If the manipulator wants that the victim asks them for things, and the victim agrees, the manipulator will only validate the desirable action with a pleasant emotional reaction sometimes. This unpredictability triggers a strong, hidden wish for good publicity on the victim's behalf, without the victim even being mindful of what is going on.

So the target can start seeking out a successful manipulator response by whatever means necessary. The manipulator makes their target behave in a certain manner so the person may have no idea what they do or why they do so. The preceding sequential technique of love bombing, positive strengthening, and finally intermittent positive reinforcement illustrates one way in which a covert emotional manipulator can deploy positive expression and cold withdrawal to sculpt their victims' emotional response. Truth denial is a strategy of CEM which initially affects the victim's mind, instead of the emotions. The effects though, as you are about to see, will devastate the feelings of a survivor.

Denying reality

One of the most painful moments a human can endure is the sense of losing his or her own sanity. This is bad enough if something obvious, such as mental disorder or the temporary by-product of pressure can explain it, but is even more unsettling if an emotional manipulator has covertly induced the feeling of madness. Reality denial applies to a variety of CEM strategies that both share the same purpose — the undermining of the conscience of a person to fulfill the personal interests of the manipulator. The ways in which the denial of reality takes place and its impact will now be further explored. Gradualism is one of the key concepts underpinning the rejection of truth. Instantly, manipulators are unlikely to strive for complete degradation of the wellbeing of a target, because such a result is difficult to accomplish without being identified. Rather, the professional manipulators appear to pursue the method "slowly but steadily." This involves the gradual erosion of a person's health until the flimsiest of foundations are placed upon their confidence in their own faculties. And how does an underhand manipulator continue the cycle of eroding the wellbeing of a victim? This often starts with small scale weakening of the confidence a person has in their own memories. The manipulator can create various circumstances where a survivor is forced to doubt their own memory of events. The manipulator must also guarantee that the one who ends up looking the most convincing is their own representation of what really occurred. This slight trust loss cycle essentially serves two overlappings, covertly deceptive ends. Second, it reduces the victim's trust in their own forces of comprehension and recollection. Next, this trust is passed over to the manipulator. It's important to remember that at first, this may never feel like a huge deal. The manipulator will literally come across with a slightly better memory as the person. The victim would be also grateful that they have somebody they can depend on for their memory!

Over time, the covert emotional manipulator will elevate the risk of the events that they cause the victim to question. What starts as innocent-looking and meaningless can be transformed into a person who lacks all faith in his own cognitive abilities. The most dangerous part of this cycle is the propensity of the survivor to blame the lack of capacity on his own mind. Professional manipulators would always be the people who manipulate the trigger so rarely make the target fully conscious of what's actually going on.

Chapter 3: Manipulation Techniques

To accomplish their ultimate aims, manipulators use bribery, mental manipulation, bringing the other individual down, deception, and building an illusion. Blackmail, lying, creating a hallucination and putting others down are the techniques used by manipulators. These are the core of every manipulators tool box so they can get the victim into doing what they want.

3.1 Blackmail

The purpose of utilizing this sort by intimidation is relying further on the subject's emotions. In regular blackmail, the target has a danger to cope with, often involving physical damage to themselves or anyone they love. For the

Emotional coercion, the manipulator must strive to evoke feelings powerful enough to motivate the victim to action. Although the target may believe they are supporting out of their own goodwill, the trickster has managed to ensure they are having the assistance and drawing out the emotions whenever required.

Blackmail is the first strategy that a trickster would use. Blackmail is deemed to be an act that involves irrational threats to make a certain benefit or cause a loss to the target unless the manipulator's demand is met. It can also be described as the act of intimidation including threats of arrest as a convict, threats of taking properties or money from the subject, or threats of physical damage to the subject. There is a long tradition of the word blackmail; initially, it was a phrase that implied payments paid by the settlers to the region surrounding Scotland to the chiefs in charge. This payment was intended to shield the settlers against the marauders and robbers that went to England.

Since then it has adapted to represent something different and in some instances, it is an offense in the U.S. For the purpose of this section, blackmail is more like a challenge to the target, whether physical or mental, to intimidate them into doing what the trickster needs.

In certain instances, Blackmail is often known to be extortion. Although there are instances when the two are typically associated, some differences do exist. Extortion, for instance, is when someone takes another's private possessions by risking to do future harm if the land is not given. In comparison, blackmail is where intimidation is used to discourage the recipient from participating in legal behavior. At times, these two things must work together. The individual will intimidate others and demand money to be held at bay to not do damage to the victim. To achieve what they want the manipulator will be able to use this tactic. They will take the chance to analyze the details of their subject of personal nature and then they will use it as a form of leverage against them. By threatening to reveal an unpleasant secret or messing their chances of having a new promotion at work, they could blackmail their target. Or the manipulator may function more threateningly by attempting to physically hurt their target or the families of the target before they decide to go along with the manipulator. Whatever the blackmail could be, it is used with the aid of the target to help the manipulator reach their final goal. And often they'll be ought to trigger the target into the action the manipulator needs. The manipulator will take advantage of the situation to get the thing they want; they will use the sympathy or remorse they excite to coerce the target into cooperating or assisting with them. Often the extent of sympathy or remorse is blown out of proportion, which makes the target even more inclined to help out in the scenario.

3.2 Putting Down the Other Person

The manipulator has other choices should they decide to persuade their target to help achieve the ultimate objective. One method that does have quite a bit of success is when the manipulator can put his subject down. For most situations, where the manipulator uses verbal skills to bring a target down, they may face a strong risk of having the subject feel as though they have been exposed to a personal assault. When the subject feels that they are being targeted, they would bristle and not be able to support the manipulator in the manner they like. We will be more careful with the procedure to find a way to do so without creating or ringing alarm bells.

One way you can achieve that is by humor. The comedy will lower obstacles which would otherwise exist because comedy is humorous and helps us feel nice. The manipulator will turn their indignation into a joke. Given the fact that the put down has transformed into a joke, it will function almost as well as though the humor were not there without creating the obvious marks on the subject. Often, the manipulator may channel their put down in the form of a 3rd person. This lets them disguise what they're doing more conveniently along with offering a simple means to refute causing damage if it comes back to haunt them. They think they are somehow smaller than the manipulator, for example. This uplifts the manipulator to a higher stage and leaves the target feeling like something needs to happen. The target is most likely to want to do it right and correct whatever errors they have made. This will bring the manipulator in a place of authority and will make it easier for them to get the target to help.

3.3 Lying

No matter what the manipulator's ultimate purpose is, lying is something they are a specialist at and can do all the time to obtain everything they want. There are many various types of lies that the manipulator will employ to help them reach their final objectives. Another being that they are spreading full lies while some are omitting portions of the facts from their targets. If the manipulator lies, it's because they realize that the lie would travel far further easily that the reality will. Telling anyone the reality could render them unable to support the manipulator out and that would go against their plans entirely. Alternatively, the manipulator would say a lie and persuade the target to do something for them because it's too late to correct the problem by the time the subject found out about the lie. The manipulator may even want to withhold some of the facts of the lies they say. They're going to say some of the reality in this approach, but they're going to leave out other details that are unsavory, or that could impede the progress being made. These types of lies can be just as hazardous as telling what the reality of the story is and what the lie becomes increasingly difficult. It's important to understand that when you're dealing with the manipulator, anything they say to you can be a lie. It's not a safe decision to believe what the manipulator does because they're only attempting to manipulate and exploit their targets to accomplish their end objective. The manipulator can do and say whatever imaginable, including lies, to get what they want and they won't feel bad for it. Because soon as they get what they want, they're not really concerned about whether it impacts the target.

3.4 Creating a Hallucination

The manipulator will not only lie but also be an expert in the creation of Illusions are more successful in achieving their ultimate target. They must try to construct a vision they like and then persuade the target that this image is really a reality; whether it matters to the manipulator or not. To achieve so, the manipulator must put up the facts required to make the argument that functions against their objective. The manipulator must plant the theories and the proof into the subject's heads to launch the deception. If these theories are in motion, the manipulator would be willing to step aside for a few days to encourage the abuse to take place in the minds of the targets during that time. By this point, the manipulator would have more opportunity to get the subject to go through with the plan. Manipulation is a type of mind control that the subject has trouble resisting. With the exception of brainwashing and hypnosis mentioned in the preceding paragraphs, deception may occur in daily life, and in certain cases, it may occur without any awareness or influence of the subject. The manipulator must operate discreetly to accomplish their end objective without making the target becoming paranoid and disrupt the operation. The manipulator won't think about who they're harming or how someone may feel because most of them won't be willing to consider their targets' needs. They only think they want something because the target they've selected would help them get to that objective. The methods mentioned throughout this chapter are intended to better illustrate what's going on throughout the manipulation phase. It's always better to seek to stay clear of someone who may be a manipulator so you can prevent this type of mind control.

Chapter 4: Emotional Influence

Our emotions lead us in our day-to-day strategic thinking, often without even noticing it. We all have primary instincts that affect our choices. While we are hungry we are searching for something to cook. When we're exhausted, we nap-or consider another cup of tea. We want to play, cuddle, or keep a little animal or new kid when we see it. These are all instinct-in-action forms of emotional reactions that impact our decisions without much additional thought.

Many influencers and marketers are familiar with all these emotional reactions and recognize when to use them to market effectively for potential customers. They use pictures and videos which inspire our emotions, make us feel pleased, comfortable, thrilled, or wanted – and not just an item, they "sell" these emotions to us. Such emotional reactions can shape our purchasing decisions.

4.1 What Is The Influence Of Emotions?

Emotional states are what gives our regular lives color: thrilled, sad, frustrated, and many more variants; and every one of these affects how we look, what we do, and yeah of course, what we purchase. And the emotions we experience once we make a choice, or buy a product will determine whether we will make that decision again. A great emotional experience can quickly generate customer loyalty or a customer who will exchange those optimistic feelings with friends, convincing more consumers to buy your product.

Marketing experts know precisely how to use these positive reactions to promote buying and keep customers coming back for the product. Find the scenario below of 2 coffee bars. Shop number one is a central cafe where you can grab a cheap doughnut and an instant cup of coffee. Shop number two has a large range of nice, though pricier, coffee varieties and options, cozy sofas, trendy music streaming, and a feel that says, "All the young kids are hanging out here." Even with the lower prices of shop number one, more customers are flocking to shop number two for the young-kid feeling and relaxing environment. This is a perfect illustration of emotional influence playing its part.

Reason emotions are so important

Although consumers may think that they use their rational mind to make choices, the reality is that many of these choices are influenced heavily by emotions. And the theory is recorded and researched well. Evidence in ads reveals that our buying decisions are more affected by the emotional responses than by the marketing material itself – often two or three times more. Other work has also used functional magnetic resonance imaging (fMRI) to demonstrate how we use our emotions to make purchasing decisions over knowledge, including evidence.

Utilize emotional influence

Ok, we know that emotional motivation is crucial to explain how decisions are made by customers, so how can we tap into that? Smart advertisers respond to these feelings by building an identity for the products. Rather than simply providing information regarding a company or business, infusing a personality gives the business life which can make it far harder to draw customers who identify with certain characteristics. From visual ads to labeling, environment, and the vocabulary used to characterize the company, these characteristics can be reflected in anything.

Forming Personas

One of the keys to understanding how emotions influence can be utilized is to create people for your final target clients. A persona is a crafted-up customer profile, which can also be outlined in the specific qualities and traits of each consumer. Having to know the people you want to approach in your branding assists you to understand customers, humanize, and help explain how to cater to their feelings.

You get a better understanding of who your targets are once

you establish the people you want to target (and yes, you can – and should – have more than one. Your online profile will include such items as age, gender, location, employment/career, relationship status, and other variables. You really should name them, and assign a stock image to them. What are their goals in life? Their points of grievances and discomfort? Their motives? Write bios for every single person you generate and you want to approach. Many of the marketing workers will use these profiles to unify the squad to ensure sure everybody is on the same page.

Marketing to your likes

You can customize your strategy when advertising your services or products once you have set up your ideal people to market to. Ask what the needs are for your character. What are their weak points, and how can your item cater to them and propose alternatives? Consider these people to be actual humans, and find some way to attract them in using their emotions.

Think further than your product, and take into account the feelings your product gives buyers. Consider how the new technology innovation makes a customer look – delighted and enthusiastic, but probably also part of a crowd "hot," clever and hip. They may be comforted to have resolved or modified a problem from an earlier version of the device. Now, you sell a way of living, not just a model, and it appeals to the emotions of your consumers. In this way, advertising sells the emotions your device provokes and will lead to increased sales success.

Initial Impression

First experiences count, whether it's to make new friends or watching a new commercial for the first time. Repeated studies show that in split seconds we establish these first impressions utilizing our intuition and emotional responses. Which is why it is so crucial to know how to advertise your product. A consumer's first exposure to an item, or its marketing, will have an instant effect on their feelings towards it and will generate favoritism in the long term.

The first feeling will be deeply emotional. Take into account using color's mental power, as well as storytelling. Motivate your consumers, help build trust, and plan a suitable product image and way of living that it supports.

Chapter 5: How You Can Use Mind Control?

The mind is the sanctuary of one individual. You can lose everything else to someone, but the sole owner of a human mind is the person itself. Absolutely correct? No!

People want to think that they have complete control over their own ideas and behaviors. That their brain is as much in control of themselves as their dominant hand is. But is that the case, really? When you're imagining, are you monitoring your dreams with care? If you can't focus, do you choose to distract your ideas? In reality, our minds are extremely sensitive to command and power. Just think about watching a scary film. The soundtrack, lighting, and camera angle choices are guiding and influencing your mind and feelings. Although you understand you're watching a film, your mind still reacts to the cues its being given. If something that we have selected and are conscious of, can impact the mind so intensely, how powerful would the impact be of a talented, dark, and psychological trickster?

5.1 Each Type of Mind Control Does Not Go Unnoticed

Undetected regulation of mind is the most dangerous form of control of the mind in nature. If somebody is aware that their brain is being impacted then cognitively, physically, or verbally they can react to it. They can prevent dealing with manipulative people. A number of people will flee to take charge at the slightest hint of a bad individual attempting to get into their head. If their mind controller is unnoticed, like a stealth bomber, then the victim cannot put up their efforts in time. There are two types of strategies to take over an undetected mind of a person — social communication, and media utilization.

Traditionally, control of the media mind was only necessary for big corporations and only relational control of mind was left to individual mind controllers. That is no longer the case, today. Computers and mobile devices have directly placed media mind manipulation powers in the hands of the coldest tricksters who walk the Earth. Before we know about the actual techniques that are used to gain undetected power over the mind, we need to think about the manipulative individuals who use these strategies. Undetected mind controllers, as with all dark psychological manipulators, have a wish to influence those around, usually for their own advantage. However, undetected mind controllers are much more lenient and practical than other manipulators. Unlike reckless psychopaths, only after careful consideration, undetected mind controllers are inclined to act. It's no simple task to manipulate someone's mind in a manner that stays undetected. It requires conscious awareness and use. Mind controllers are cautious and clever creatures, regardless of that. They also worry about being spotted out so they target to hide as much as possible of their techniques. They're like secret puppet masters, pulling the strings of their victims from behind a veil.

5.2 Undetected Tactics of Mind Control

Let's understand about the particular methods manipulators

use to regulate an undetected way of thinking of a victim. We will discover the interpersonal and television techniques which constitute the toolkit of a manipulator. Examples of how these strategies may be used on a person or larger collective scale will be given.

Finding the Victim

One of the first and most significant psychological concepts of undetected regulation of mind is to identify a victim with a goal. Scientifically as well as anecdotally, it has been proven that an individual with an urgent need or desire is more vulnerable to unrecognized control of the mind than someone who feels at ease and comfortable. This can range from a simple, physical target like feeling thirsty and wanting a drink to a big, psychological objective like needing love and affection. Reckon of someone in a crowd seeking someone else. They'll succeed in filtering out all the people who aren't their goal and fine-tune the one who is. The brain is akin to that. If there is something that it wants or needs, it can direct an individual toward it, even if they are unsure that there is any control going on. The greatest mind controllers will distinguish discreetly what the goals of a victim are, and will try to manipulate people with these goals in mind. One textbook example of the vulnerability of people with a target is a subliminally conditioned experiment. Subliminal influence is yet another term for undetected control of the mind. A movie with a hidden picture of an iced tea was shown to two sets of people. One group of people was thirsty, but the other was not. When given the chance to buy a particular drink from a collection, the thirsty people purchased the iced tea in larger numbers than numerically would have been anticipated. This is proof that when a person's brain becomes hungry for something, it would happily come up with ideas of what to pick. So how does that principle work on an interpersonal, individual scale? If a mind controller discovers a victim who craves something desperately in their life, usually the satisfaction of some deep emotional need, the manipulator will be capable of controlling their mind more easily. For starters, if a person has recently experienced a breakdown of a romantic partnership, it is possible that their psychology is needing a friend. The mind controller will impact their victim into thinking they are the hero of the victim when they are probable to be their ruin in truth. Some of the most common spaces of need for a manipulator to exploit will include a person's need for monetary stability, their need for belonging, and their need for friends. An experienced manipulator can exploit these vulnerabilities for a range of purposes. The manipulator may try to exploit their victim, either sexually or economically. They may seek to gain loyalty to some form of cult or extreme ideological movement. For their own sadistic pleasure, they may simply toy with the victim.

Restricting selection

Restricting options is an undetected spoken method of mind regulation. It's a really sophisticated type of dark manipulation, as it offers a number of built-in "get out provisions" for the manipulator should their target become suspicious. The best approach to this specific form of mind control is to remove any real choice a victim has about a specific circumstance while creating an illusion that the victim has been in control all the time. The choice restriction is comparable to a common and effective selling strategy known as a close option. I will use a way to show this process, correctly identifying the distinction between somebody behaving in a psychologically normal manner and a dark manipulator who only wants to satisfy their own motive at the cost of others. Take a lady who's getting asked out for a date. A regular guy might be brave enough to ask his question, lacking confidence or surety, and finally stammering out an open-ended question like "Do you want to go out with me?" "Such a query leaves a clear chance for a" No "response. This is the standard way things go for people unfamiliar with the use of dark psychology rules. However, somebody who knows how to control somebody's mind in an undetected way will engage in the same situation quite differently. They like to tempt their victim with confidence and smoothness, to get them to chuckle and to lower their guard. Then, the manipulator will ask with complete confidence and assurance "So, am I taking you out on Wednesday or Sunday night?" The restricted choice given to the victim, who because of the elegance is in a mentally soft state, will mostly result in the victim selecting between Wednesday or Sunday night. Answering 'no' has never been a choice. The devilish aspect of the above method is that there is no real evidence of the words an individual has spoken, unlike many other forms of mind manipulation, including those assisted by the media. If the victim, miraculously, picks up on the manipulator's restriction of options, the manipulator can react in two ways — a rejection or reconstruct. A rejection allows the manipulator to insist that they do not offer a limited selection and that the victim memorizes things incorrectly or is too concerned. A reconstruct can allow the manipulator to put the victim on the rear leg by saying something like "I can't believe you're doing so much analysis of my words. This really hurts me and makes me unwilling to open up to you. "Both the rejection and the reconstruct are effective emergency escape strategies for the spotted manipulator.

5.3 Mind Control through Pictures

As the five senses in life are our guidance, so too can they be our opponents and traitors. Our sense of sight and the brain's visual processing facilities are very potent. We almost always fantasize visually, even if there is a lack of a different sense, and we generally picture anyone we remember, instead of aligning some other sensory input. This allows imagery and mental distortion an especially effective media mind management tool. Advertising development has historically remained in the possession of institutions and corporations. These deceptive forces were able to advance the creation of visual, subliminal influence of thought. Examples include split-second images of a product or person being inserted into an apparently innocent film. These split-second photos, which the viewer perceives as nothing but a blur of light, are capable of taking effective control of the emotions of an individual. They were used just as recently as presidential elections of the 21st century. These devastatingly effective imaging methods are in the control of individual manipulators now, worryingly. To make matters worse, these strategies may now be adapted to a single person. If the victim has a specific fear of something or avoidance of it, the manipulator can use the frightening image subtly to access and distort the emotions of a person without knowing. Let's consider the example of individual mind control with imagery. We are living in the Mobile and Video era. Everything at the contact of a screen can shoot full HD clips and deliver them to others at blistering speeds. Therefore, high-tech manipulators can refer to images that are feared. For instance, if a manipulative husband is conscious that his wife is deeply afraid of insects, during a video chat, he may "mistakenly" place a book with an insect image on its cover in the background. The wife is unlikely to deliberately register the position of the book but she will feel its effect on a delicate, emotional level.

5.4 Mind Control through Sound

Sound is another way a person is prone to untraceable control of his or her mind. That will be confirmed to you by both studies and personal observations. Have you ever felt that a song I stuck in your mind? Is it easy to get rid of it? Even though you realized it was present, the audio had a strong influence over you. When it is undetected the strength of audio manipulation becomes even greater. Studies have shown that if cafe customers are introduced to music from a given area, there are more chances that they will order wine from that country. When asked they had no clue that their choice had been steered by something as basic as sound. The cowering of words and expressions in music as well as other media that contain background music is one renowned example of media mind manipulation using sound. There have been court cases aimed at proving that performers in their work conceal occult references, and to restrict them from doing so. That has also occurred beyond the television media world, with a more significant impact. Audio mind manipulation is often used by governments as a form of brainwashing. In North Korea for example, people are forced to listen regularly to patriotic songs. These are deeply embedded within a person's mindset and affect an unknown influence. Think commercial jingles, for a less serious illustration. If a person is triggered by a popular jingle's song, such as the melody of the McDonald's "I'm loving it," the individual normally repeats on autopilot the promotional message. Specific manipulators can often utilize the audio undetected mind power. There are a number of techniques of behavioral manipulation utilizing different forms of auditory mind regulation. Even if you understand the strategies, you still have difficulty recognizing that they are being implemented. This is because of their sneaky, submissive nature. One of the creepiest forms of audible mind control is to unconsciously influence a person as he sleeps. Have you ever seen such CDs and videos that are used to help people avoid smoking through sleep? The evil equivalent of such products is an experienced mind controller. The manipulator will take this opportunity to inject their gloomy and deceitful commands into a person's ear and let them submerge into the deepest part of the brain when a victim is at its most vulnerable when they totally let their guard down by falling asleep. The masking of phrases with similar-sounding phrases or noises is yet another form of interpersonal auditory mind control. Have you seen the movie American Psycho? Though it is fiction, it shows true methods of mind control. The main character, serial killer Patrick Bateman, openly informs his targets what he is doing: "I am in executions and murders." When confronted about what he said, he answers simply, "I am in acquisitions and mergers." The subliminal effect is already in the psychological recesses of the individual. Sounds outside the spectrum of human hearing are a type of auditory mind regulation and can be utilized by both individuals and organizations. Such sounds, which are specific frequencies, instill deep fear, dread, or uneasiness to those who are unintentionally exposed to them. Although widely used in horror movies, such sounds have been successfully used by some innovative mind controllers to impact their victims' emotional stability and well-being.

Chapter 6: Persuasion Techniques

The problem with this method is that there are often so many various types of persuasion found in daily life that it can be impossible for anyone person to reach through to the target and create a change. While persuasion serves to alter the target's thinking and perceptions like the other types of mind regulation, it feels as though everyone is attempting to convince you over something such that it is easier to resist the suggestion that comes to the target. For instance, when an argument is going on, the advertisements on television, or even when a debate is going on, a sort of convincing is taking place. People also use persuasion without knowing, to their benefit. This chapter would go into more depth on persuasion and how it can be used successfully as a method of mind control.

6.1 What Is Persuasion?

We start with the concept of persuasion. As people talk of persuasion, several specific responses can also come up. Some might think about the ads and advertising they see all over them that promote the buying of a certain commodity over another. Some might think about political persuasion and how the politicians might seek to manipulate the decision of the people in order to have another vote. Both are forms of persuasion because the message attempts to change the way the subject thinks. Persuasion will be seen in daily life and it's a very strong tool and has a huge influence on the topic and culture. Advertisement, mainstream media, legal rulings, and policy can also be affected by how persuasion functions which in effect will attempt to persuade the target as well. In order to transform their attitudes and personality, brainwashing and hypnosis would require the victim to remain in solitude. Coercion will also operate with only one individual to achieve the ultimate target. While persuasion can be executed on just one target to change their minds, it is also achievable to use persuasion on a wider scale to persuade a whole community or even society to think differently. This can make it all the more effective and potentially fatal because it has the opportunity to alter many people's minds in one go instead of just a single subject's mind. Moreover, most subjects should be able to resist the advertisements for purchasing TV and luxury vehicles or the newest item in the market. Other occasions the method of manipulation can be even more discreet so it will be more challenging for the target to shape their own views on what they are being informed. They'll think about a dealer or conman who's attempting to get them to alter all their values and who'll pressure and annoy them before the transition happens. While that is definitely one form of talking about convincing, it is also important to use this method in a constructive manner instead of just a negative. For starters, public service ads may persuade citizens to avoid smoking or recycle and provide convincing ways that will enhance the subject's existence. It's all about how the convincing process is used.

What is persuasion composed of?

As for the other methods of mind regulation, when it comes to persuasion, there are some things to look out for. These elements help define exactly what persuasion is to make it more acknowledged. Persuasion is described as "a symbolic mechanism in which communications attempt to encourage certain people to alter their attitudes or behaviors about a problem by transmitting a message in a free-choice environment."

It is one of the aspects that separate persuasion from the other methods of mind control; the individual is always able to make their own informed decisions about the matter, regardless of the fact that persuasion techniques are going to work to move the mind of the individual in a certain direction. Whether they choose to purchase a product or not, or whether they believe the reasoning behind the argument is compelling enough to shift their minds, the respondent will choose which way they want to believe. There are a few aspects found in the persuasion that help to better describe it. These factors include: persuasion is visual because it includes noises, pictures, and phrases to bring the point across. Persuasion requires the person to actively seeking to persuade the target or community. Self-persuasion is a central aspect of the face, web, radio, and television. The communication may also take place either verbally or nonverbally. Let's look in a little more depth at each of these issues. The first factor of convincing is that a symbolic picture is necessary.

To persuade others, you ought to be willing to convince them that they can adjust their mindset, or behave in a certain way. It will involve utilizing phrases, sounds, and pictures to communicate the new message. To prove your case, you will use the terms to launch a discussion or statement. Pictures are a great way of showing the evidence needed to convince someone to go one way or the other. Few non-verbal cues are available, but they would not be as successful as utilizing the words and pictures. The second point is that manipulation should be done in a calculated manner to affect how people behave or think. This one is fairly simple, if you don't want to Influence others deliberately, you don't use coercion to alter them. The persuader will use various strategies to convince the target to believe the same way they do. This may be as easy as either holding a conversation with them or providing facts that confirm their perspective. But on the other side, it could get a lot more involved and consist of more complicated ways to alter the mind of the victim. Much of the methods utilized in persuasion will be addressed later in this segment. The interesting aspect of persuasion is that it provides a sort of free will to the target. The victim should make his / her own decision in the manner. For the most part, they do not have to go for it, no matter how hard somebody tries to convince them for something. The topic may listen to a thousand advertisements on the best car to purchase, but if they don't want that model or don't need a new automobile then they won't go out and purchase one. If the person is against abortion, how many individuals come out and say how big abortion is won't matter, the participant is unlikely to change their minds. This enables much more free choice than is found in the other aspects of mind manipulation, which could demonstrate why when asked, many people don't see this as a kind of mind control. Persuasion is a type of mind control that can take place in a variety of different ways. While brainwashing, hypnosis and manipulation must occur face-to-face, and sometimes in total secrecy, persuasion is unable to occur otherwise. Examples of persuasion can be found all over the place. For several years Persuasion has been around; in reality, it has been around since ancient Greece.

That doesn't suggest the craft and reasoning methods are just the same as they were back then. In reality, quite a few modifications have been introduced to the art of persuasion, and how it is used in present society. This section will look at the key elements of modern-day persuasion. Richard M. Perl off spent a good amount of time researching new manipulation, how it is being done, and how it will influence the entire society. He has written a novel, The Persuasion Dynamics.

Communication and behavior of the twenty-first century, and describes the five aspects in which the application of contemporary persuasion is distinct from those used in the past. Such five forms include: The amount of communications found convincing has increased by leaps and bounds.

The argument was seen in ancient Greece's times only in literature and in elite debates. Convincing was not a major deal so you wouldn't see that too much. In modern days, taking you around is hard without any sign of persuasion. Think about the different methods and forms of commercials out there; the average person in the U.S. will find up to 3000 of these every day. Besides that, there are always people banging at your door trying to get you to purchase something, believe their suggestions, or try something new. Persuasion is far more a part of modern life than it has been in the past at any other time. Persuasion moves really fast: back in ancient Greece periods, it might take months or longer to get from one point to another for a persuasive message. This restricted the effect of persuasion since most people could not get the signal. Most actions of persuasion had political candidates reach constituents in just secs at once and any message can be quickly transmitted. Persuasion takes on a much greater role when it can spread so fast.

Persuasion can imply a great deal of money: now that businesses have uncovered the influence of persuasion, they are doing whatever they can to make it work. The more effective they are in convincing customers to purchase their goods the more money they receive.

Some businesses solely exist due to the persuasive system, such as public relations firms, marketing companies, and advertising companies. Other firms will be able to use the persuasive methods offered by these firms to reach and exceed the sales goals they set. Persuasion has become cleverer than in history: at the start of persuasion, the operator would announce their viewpoints loudly for the whole group to listen in the hope of getting them all to change their opinions. These days are gone as the method of convincing has become even more discrete. While it is common to see actions of convincing that are often very overt and in your face, like with certain types of advertisement, many others take a more discreet route. An indication of that is where companies build a certain impression of themselves, such as being nice to the customer, in order to encourage people to purchase the product. You might also note that instead of participating in a conversation with your mate about going to a dance, they're trying to use social pressure or maybe mention a few things to try to convince you to come along. Despite being more sophisticated, persuasion is just as useful today as it has ever been. The persuasion process has become more and they have to make many more decisions. For example, when previously a person has only gone to the one supermarket in town to purchase anything they need, now they can choose from various shops for their requirements from the hardware store to the food store to the clothes store. Besides this, there is also more than one choice available in the area for any of these consumer categories. All those choices make it harder for the operator to find a strong message of persuasion for the customer or some other topic.

6.2 Different Ways to Persuade Someone

Techniques of persuasion may also fall under certain terms and are referred to in forms such as tactics of persuasion and techniques of persuasion. There is not just one approach that can be used to convince someone to believe or to behave in any way. The operator may be able to discuss the matter while submitting proof in order to change the mind of the target, they may be able to use some kind of force or pull against a target, and may offer the target a favor, or use another tactic.

Using Power

Depending on the context, the agent can conclude that using

certain coercion to get the target to think that way is a good idea. This can happen when the ideas don't match accurately, the regular conversation doesn't work, or when the operator becomes frustrated or annoyed where the conversation is going. Often force is used as a sort of fear tactic as it gives the target less time to rationally think about what happens particularly in comparison to when a reasonable discussion takes place. Generally, a force can be used when the operator has had less effectiveness using the other available modes of persuasion, although sometimes it is also done starting with the use of power. At other times, the force can be used when the operator feels like they are losing track or when the target is capable of presenting counter-evidence to the operator and the operator becomes angry. It is often not the smartest choice to use force when it comes to feeling more likely to be in danger. If the target is challenged, they're less willing to respond and hear something the operator does, and the cycle won't move forward. Due to all of these factors the usage of coercion in the practice of persuasion is usually prohibited and avoided; unlike the other methods of mind regulation mentioned.

Tactics of influence

Another technique that can be used to convince the target to lean a particular way is to utilize the available weapons of influence. Robert Cialdini developed those six influences in his book Influence. This book explores the art of convincing and describes the six tools of control that will render the person effective with their aims. Reciprocity, loyalty and continuity, social verification, interest, power, and scarcity are the six tools of control. Such six tools of control are very important to the operator because they are a part of their targets' shift mechanism. Each of these six arms will be addressed below. Reciprocity The concept of reciprocity is the first tool of power. The theory implies that if one person, the operator, gives anything of interest to the other party, the target, and then the subject must seek to compensate the agent in return. It simply implies that, as the agent provides a sort of service to the target, the target may believe that at that stage they have a duty to provide a comparable service to the agent. Although the two services will not be equivalent, they have the same kind of meaning such that the responsibility to both is equal. The rule of reciprocity is very effective because it helps the agent get the subject into the right frame of mind for the act of persuasion by quieting and overpowering the subject with a sense of duty. The agent may be more likely to convince the subject to do or act in some way because the subject will have that sense of duty hanging over them. The agent won't have to think over whether the target should have the correct moral code to have transform the favor. Unless the subject will not feel the need to do so,

---

the investigator should have certain means at their fingertips to drive it into action. Yet when it was required the topic never gave it back. Now, by telling the favor, the agent has forced social standards on the subject, making it even more likely that they will be able to persuade the subject to do something. For the most part, the subject will be happy to reciprocate with the agent without needing any outside forces. When the favor is granted, the subject will begin to look for ways to repay the agent so that the score is even and they don't appear greedy or selfish. The agent will then be able to provide the subject with an easy solution on how to repay the debt; the subject will feel gratitude for having this easy solution and will be more likely to go the way the agent wants.

Consistency and engagement

The next weapon of influence to be debated is engagement and consistency. If they want to persuade anybody to change their perspective, the operator will need to use these. When things seem to be consistent, they are simpler to comprehend and can help the target make better decisions. It's not fair for the operator to constantly adjust the details they're using, or alter any things required to support the target interpret the evidence. Instead of helping the

Mechanism of persuasion, always moving away from continuity, can render the negotiator appear like a thief and someone who cannot be believed, culminating in the collapse of the method of persuasion. Continuity is one of the most critical facets of the process of persuasion.

Consistency is widely respected in society: people want stuff to continue a particular way much of the time. Although there is a lot of variation in daily life, people are comfortable ensuring that stuff should be fairly stable generally.

This helps us to understand what has occurred, to know what to expect, and to be informed should any adjustments arise. When continuity was not present, it would be very difficult to schedule anything and there would still be confusing problems running on. When you decide to persuade a person about a certain topic, so you have to be sure that the statements are clear and important to them.

Feeling consistently like a disaster. People prefer continuity as it allows them to recognize when to do and when to do. We recognize what it's time to sleep when it's time to function, and what those items are going to happen all day long. Consistency provides a really useful shortcut, due to the complications present in modern existence. Life is complicated enough without contributing to certain items that don't make sense. When individuals will have stable lives, it makes it even easier. Consistency is a wonderful asset since it helps the person to make the best choices and manage knowledge. When the operator wants to be effective in their efforts to convince the target, they must guarantee that their argument is accurate. There is little space for misleading proof that could then surface to spoil the whole operation. Hold the evidence accurately and descriptive to convince the subject easily.

The process of communication is one that blends in with continuity. It is necessary to have a sort of agreement in order and recognize that the target is genuinely convinced and that the initiative has paid off. In advertising, this can imply that the subject will buy a product or in elections, it can mean that a target will vote for a specific candidate. The commitment made will vary according to the type of persuasion.

As per the concept of consistency, if a person commits, either in writing or orally, they are far more prone to uphold the commitment they have made. It's been discovered that this is even more accurate in case of written agreements since the target will be psychologically more specific and there will be some hard evidence that they agreed to the commitment. That makes good sense; many people are going to guarantee orally that they are going to fix or do something, only to flip around. Sure, some people are going to do what they say and they are more probable to do that if promising verbally than not promising whatsoever, but often it's still hard to get the outcomes you want in that way. Moreover, there's no way to back up that claim as an oral agreement just becomes a disagreement he said she said and no one will eventually win. From the other side, if the operator could get a written promise, the target can move ahead to continue participating in self-persuasion for the purpose.

They must have numerous justifications and explanations for supporting the undertaking along with others to prevent any problems with the operator. If the operator can bring the target to that level the agent would have even less research to do.

Social proof

Persuasion is a means of social contact, and so the social rules, when it happens, would have to be observed. The subject will be influenced by the people around them; they will be more likely to want to do what everyone else is doing, instead of doing their own thing. The subject will base their actions and beliefs on what others do around them, how they behave, and how they think. For instance, if the target grows up in a neighborhood, they are more apt to behave like people from that neighborhood; on the other side, those who grow up in a very religious society will invest a lot of their time studying, educating, and supporting others. Under this belief, the phrase "the crowd's influence" may be very powerful. The target will want to understand what individuals around them do all the time. In this world, it has become almost an addiction to be willing to follow what others are doing and fit in, considering the idea that individuals are trying to tell that they choose to be special and be an individual. An explanation that is offered of whether people are going to do things if others are doing something can be seen on a phone a thon. If the host says something like "Operators are waiting, please call now," then the subject might feel like there are operators sitting around doing nothing because nobody is calling them. That would make the target less apt to respond because they feel that if no one will call then they will not call either. If the host changes just a few words and instead says "If operators are preoccupied, try calling again," a really different outcome can be achieved. The target will now believe that the operators are preoccupied with many other targets' calls so the company must be nice and valid. The target will be much more inclined to contact in if they get through immediately or have to be put on hold. The method of persuasion of social proof is by far the most accurate in scenarios where the target is unsure of what they are going to do or where there appear to be many resemblances in the situations. The topic would always prefer to adhere to what people around them are doing in unclear or unpredictable circumstances that involve several decisions or options to make. This is because of the way it should be. If there is anyone similar to the subject in charge, the subject will probably listen to them and follow them more than if the person in charge is very different from the subject. The operator will be able to use the idea of social proof to help with their art of persuasion. The first way they will do this is to

analyze the language they speak.

Chapter 7: Understanding Deception

Deception means the act— huge or small, toxic, or kind— of motivating followers to accept data that is not true. Lying is a popular type of deception — the statement of something identified to be false with the intention of deceiving.

Though most people are usually honest, there are times when even those who adhere to honesty participate in deception. Research suggests the typical citizen lies multiple times each day. Some of such lies are major ("I've never betrayed you!") but more frequently than not, they are tiny white lies ("That suit looks perfectly fine") employed to escape awkward circumstances or to protect the sentiments of someone.

7.1 Forms of Deception

Trust is the foundation stone of all types of social life, from the love story and parental involvement to government. This is often compromised by deceit. Since truth is so necessary for human company, which focuses on a common vision of reality, most individuals have the general assumption that everyone else is sincere in their connectivity and dealings. Many traditions have strict societal prohibitions against deception.

There are several forms of deception which may occur. There are 5 specific forms of deceit discovered, according to the Interpersonal Deception Theory. Some of these have been demonstrated in other aspects of mind control, showing that some overlap can occur. The 5 major types of deception usually involve:

Lies: this is where the operator makes up information or offers data that is totally opposite from what the reality is. This information will be presented to the target as fast and the target will see it as the reality. It may be risky because the subject is not likely to know that they are being given fake facts; if the target realized the facts were inaccurate, they would certainly not speak to the operator and there would be no deceit.

Equivocations: this is where the agent renders comments which are inconsistent, vague, or conditional. This is executed to lead the target into confusion and not to know what's happening. It could also help the operator to save face when the target returns later and wants to accuse them for the misinformation.

Concealments: This is one of the most prevalent forms of deceit used. Conceals are when the operator omits data useful or relevant to the setting, or they purposely engage in any conduct that would hide the information relevant to the target for that specific context. The operator may not have lied explicitly to the issue, but they would have assumed that the crucial knowledge that is required will never reach the target.

Exaggeration: this is where the agent overestimates an aspect that twists the facts a little, to transform the narrative the way they want. While the operator may not be telling lies directly to the target, they are trying to do the complete opposite of the method of exaggeration in that the operator will understate or lessen elements of the reality. They'll tell the target that an incident isn't that big deal when it could actually be the factor that defines whether the target gets to graduate or gets a very nice raise. The operator will be ready to look back later saying how they didn't even realize how big of a deal it was, letting them look good and the target looks just about petty if they whine. These are all just a few of the kinds of deception that could be found. The operator of the deception will use any method available to them to reach their ultimate goal, much like what happens in the other types of mind control. If they can accomplish their target using another approach against the target, then they can do so and the above list is not unique in any way. The deceit operator will be very harmful as the target may not be able to recognize what the reality is and what is an act of manipulation; the operator may be so experienced at what they are doing that it would be nearly difficult to decide what is the reality and what is not.

7.2 Reasons for Deceit

Researchers have shown that three major motivations are

involved in deceptions detected in close ties. These would involve motives focused on partners, motives focused on oneself, and motives fixated on relationships.

Let's look at the motivations that centered on the partner first. In such a motive, the operator may use deceit to prevent hurting the subject or his spouse. They can even use the manipulation to secure the subject's friendship with an unknown third party or prevent having the target worry about something, or hold the subject's self-esteem preserved. This kind of deception ambition will often be seen as both relationally beneficial and socially friendly. This kind of deception is not as terrible as some of the others. If the operator learns something negative that the best friend of the subject says about them, then the operator may choose to hold it to self. Although this is a type of deceit, it lets the target preserve the relationship thus preventing the target from feeling sorry for itself. This is the most commonly noticed type of deceit in partnerships, which does not do too much harm if it is detected. Most couples would want to think of their own self-image and also how they feel. In this intent, the operator uses the deception to safeguard or enhance its own image. This method of deceit is used to protect the person from scrutiny, humiliation, or frustration. Typically, when this manipulation is utilized in the partnership, it is viewed as being a more serious problem and transgression as compared to the partner-focused deception. It is because the operator chooses to act in a selfish manner rather than acting to protect the marriage or another partner. The operator will use this deception with the aim of restricting any damage that could come to the relationship simply by ignoring the distress and dispute in relation. This type of deceit, depending on the circumstance, often benefits the relationship while at other times it can be the source of hurting the relationship as it can make it more difficult. For e.g., if you want to mask how you feel about dinner because you don't want to get into a confrontation, the relationship might benefit from it. But on the other side, if you have an affair and instead choose to keep this story to yourself, it will ultimately only make the situation more complicated.

It doesn't matter what the deception is intended for, it is not recommended in a relationship. The operator holds knowledge that might be relevant to the target; if the target finds out about it, they tend to lose faith in the operator and question what else the operator is withholding from them. And for the purpose behind the deceit, the target won't be too worried, they'll just be frustrated that something has been kept as a secret from them and that the relationship will start to break. Often it's better to adhere to the relationship's loyalty strategy and associate yourself with others who don't pursue deceit in your social circle.

7.3 Monitoring Deception

If the person is involved in preventing deceit throughout their life to prevent the games of mind that come with it, it is always a smart thing to know how to recognize deception as it occurs. The target often finds it hard to determine that deception occurs unless the operator slips up and either says a lie that is evident or outrageous or contradicts something that the target already knows is accurate. While it may be challenging for the operator to deceive the target for a long period of time, it is something that will usually happen between individuals who know one another in daily life. Identifying when deceit happens is always challenging, as there are often no ways to say when deceit happens that are absolutely accurate. Owing to the pressure of holding the tale correct, the operator is often more prone to spill details to alert the target by either verbal or non - verbal or verbal signals. Researchers claim that identifying deceit is a perceptual, dynamic, and nuanced mechanism that also differs based on the communication being shared. The actions of the operator will be interconnected with the actions taken by the target after receiving the message. During this swap, the operator will expose the visual and verbal information that will pinpoint the deceit to the target. At some places, the target may be able to say that the operator lied to them.

When the operator is being dishonest, it's not always easy to say. According to Warn Vrij, a renowned researcher of deceit, there are no especially correlated nonverbal conducts of deceit. Although there are some nonverbal actions that may be associated with the act of deceit, such signals may often appear while certain activities are occurring, and it becomes impossible to decide if the person utilizes deception until they commit a direct lie. Another researcher of deceit, Mark Frank, offers another definition of manipulation that involves whether it may be identified at the emotional level of the participant. When there is deception, it needs mindful conduct that is intentional on the part of the operator so listening to phrase and paying enough attention to the body language and facial expressions that are going on are both crucial when trying to determine if someone is misleading you. If someone poses a question and the operator is not prepared to answer it directly, instead of using some type of disruption, has an inadequate logic structure, keeps repeating words a lot, he is probably lying. There are some non-verbal signs that may be visible when someone is misleading, but they may also have some other issues like anxiety or shyness. These are components that will be recognized later if the operator uses the deception process in the correct manner. Camouflage, disguise, and illusion are the three primary elements of deceit.

Camouflage

Camouflage is the first element of deceit. That's when the operator works to conceal the facts in a different way so that the target does not understand that the information is missing. This method will often be employed when the operator uses half-truths when they tell details. The target will not recognize that the camouflaging took place until afterward when these facts are in some way disclosed. The operator will be talented in camouflaging the reality so that by chance the possibility of target finding out about deception is really difficult.

Disguise

Disguise is yet another element that can be observed in the deception procedure. When this happens, the operator works to create an impression that he is something or someone else. That is where the operator masks everything about himself from the target, such as his real name, what they do for a career, who they were with, and what they are up to when they're out. This extends beyond just altering the costume that someone wears in a play or film; while disguise is utilized in the process of deception, the actor tries to alter their whole appearance to confuse and manipulate the target. There are many scenarios that may explain the usage of disguise in the cycle of deception. The first is disguising themselves in relationships with the operator, usually as another individual so that they cannot be recognized. This could be achieved by the operator to get back into a pool of people who don't like them, alter their personality to have others like them, or for some purpose to fulfill their objectives. The term disguise can in certain situations apply to the operator disguising the true essence of a plan in the hopes of avoiding an influence or motive incompatible with that request. Often this type of disguise is noticed in propaganda or politics because it hides the real nature of what is happening. If the agent hides who they are from the target, then it can be very hard for the target to assess who they really are. When data is withheld from the target, it clouds the way they can think because they do not have the correct knowledge to make rational decisions. While the target may think they make rational decisions of their own free will, the operator has taken away critical details that can change the mind of the target.

Simulation

The third part of the deception is called simulation. This comprises of displaying false information to the target. There are 3 methods that could be used in the simulation, such as distraction, fabrication, and imitation.

In mimicry, or imitating another system, the operator will unconsciously portray something similar to itself. They may have an idea similar to somebody else's and instead of giving credit, they're going to say it's all theirs. Sometimes this type of stimulation may occur by auditory, visual, and other means.

Fabrication is yet another tool that can be used by the operator while using deception. What this implies is that the operator takes something found in actuality and changes it to make it different. They could tell a story that hasn't happened or add adornments that make it look better or worse than it actually was. Whereas the center of the story may well be true, yes they got a bad grade on a test, it's going to have some modification like the teacher deliberately gave them a failing grade. The truth is that the operator did not study and that's the reason they got the bad grade in the first place. Ultimately, distraction is yet another type of deception simulation. This is when the operator tries to get the target to concentrate on something other than the reality; generally by baiting or providing something that could be more enticing than the concealed reality. For instance, if the husband cheats and feels the wife is beginning to find out, he might carry a diamond ring home to divert her from the problem for a brief moment.

The problem with this method is that it often doesn't last long and the agent has to find other ways of deceiving the target to keep the process going.

Chapter 8: Seduction Techniques

It all depends on the victim of your seduction. Analyze your prey extensively, and select only those that will prove vulnerable to your enchantments. The right targets are the ones you can fill in a void for, who see something unusual in you. They are mostly isolated or miserable, or they can be quickly made so — because it's almost impossible to seduce an entirely contented person. The right target has a certain quality that triggers intense emotions within you, making your seductive moves seem more normal and fluid. A perfect target allows ideal pursuit.

8.1 Seduction Tool Kit

Generate a greater sense of safety

"If you're too plain forward early on, you risk building up a resentment that's never going to be extinguished. At first nothing of the seducer has to be in your form. The seduction should start at an angle, not directed straight so that the target only becomes aware of you slowly. Haunt the outskirts of the existence of your target — approach via a third party, or appear to develop a fairly neutral connection, progressively moving from colleague to lover. Lure the target into feeling safe, then strike.

Appear to be a desired object-create triangles

"Few are drawn to the individual evaded and neglected by others; crowds gather around those that have already lured interest. In order to attract your victims to make them desperate to have you, you need to create an illusion of desirability — of being needed by many. Being the favored object of your interest will make them happy, to win your heart in an audience of admirers. Make a reputation that precedes you: There must be a reason if many have failed to resist your charms.

Sending out mixed signals

"Once individuals are conscious of your presence, and maybe slightly fascinated, you ought to spice up the curiosity before it falls on another person. Most of us are way too obvious — be difficult to sort out, instead. Send confusing messages: harsh and delicate, both religious and worldly, harmless as well as devious. A mixture of characteristics suggests depth, which also fascinates as much as it confuses. A mysterious, mystical atmosphere can make people crave more knowledge and pull them towards you. Generate such authority by suggesting something conflicting within you.

Creating need

"It is almost impossible to seduce a person who is perfectly satisfied. You need to instill tension and disharmony in your target's mind. Stir up feelings of dissatisfaction within them, resentment with their conditions, and with themselves. The sense you create of inferiority will give you the space to assert yourself, to start making them see you as the solution to their issues. Pain and fear are the right predecessors of satisfaction. Learn how to produce the need you can fill up.

Step into their minds

"Most individuals are locked into their own realms, which makes them stubborn and difficult to persuade. Moving into their soul is the way to draw them out of their isolation and set up the seduction. Live by their guidelines, have fun doing what they love, adjust to their feelings. You will massage their deep-rooted narcissism and reduce their defenses in doing so. Take part in every move and whim of your targets, offering them nothing at all to react against or resist.

Master the technique of conceit

"It's important to make your targets feel frustrated and require your help, but if you're too clear, they'll see through you and become defensive. However, there is no established protection against insinuation — the art of injecting ideas in the heads of individuals by dropping hints which take hold days later, sometimes looking to them as their real concept. Develop a sublanguage — big claim accompanied by discharge and apology, vague comments, banal conversation combined with seductive glances — that enters the unconscious of the target

to express your true meaning. Get it all provocative.

Generate Temptation

"Tempt the victim deep into your seduction by building the perfect temptation: a glance of the delights to arrive. As the serpent persuaded Eve with the guarantee of prohibited knowledge, you must generate an urge in your targets that they cannot govern. Discover their weak spot, that fantasy that has yet to be understood, and indicate that you can lead them toward it.

Use the devilish power of words to generate confusion

Convincing people to listen is hard; they are filled by their own opinions and needs, so they have no patience for yours. The way to make them care is to suggest whatever they want to know, flooding their ears with anything they want. This is the core of seductive words. Use loaded words to stir up feelings, flatter them, comfort their anxieties, envelop them with lovely words and promises, and not only will they pay attention to you, but they will also end up losing their will to oppose you.

Holding them in anticipation- what's next?

"The moment people believe they know what to anticipate from you, the hold over them is shattered. More: You have lost power over them. The best way to control the seduced and retain the advantage is to build anticipation, a measured shock. Attempting something they don't anticipate from you would offer them a wonderful feeling of spontaneity — they won't be able to predict what's next.

Look out for information

"Lofty expressions of affection and nice movements may be suspicious: why are you striving so hard to impress? The nuances of a seduction — the discreet movements, the offhand stuff you do — are much more enticing and surprising. You have to learn to confuse your victims with a multitude of fun little routines — personalized presents suited to them, clothing, and accessories crafted to satisfy them, actions that demonstrate the time and energy you are giving them.

Make your presence felt

"Significant stuff happens when the victims are alone: the faintest sense of relief in your absence and the whole plan goes in vain. Predictability and over-exposure will trigger this response. Stay mysterious, then. Intrigue your victims by varying a thrilling existence with a nice distance, joyful instances accompanied by computed absences.

Relate yourself with romantic pictures and items, so they continue to see you as a charming person. The more you figure out what's in their minds, the greater the seductive illusions they wrap you in.

Confuse need and reality

People spend a lot of their time dreaming, envisioning a future full of wonder, achievement, and romance to accommodate the challenges in their lives. If you are able to develop the illusion that they can live their fantasies out via you, you will get them at your grace. Target at secret desires that have been thwarted or silenced, inflame inexplicable emotions, cloud their reasoning powers. Lead the seduced to a stage of confusion where they can't distinguish between illusion and reality anymore.

Disarm through tactical weakness and insecurity

Far too much maneuvering on your aspect can give rise to distrust. The finest way to hide your paths is to make the person look special and powerful. If you seem to be feeble, vulnerable, enthusiastic about the other individual, and unable to regulate yourself, you will make your conduct look quite natural, less orchestrated. Lack of strength — crying, bashfulness, pale skin — will help to build the influence.

Victim isolation

A lonely individual becomes fragile. Through gradually isolating the victims, you render them more prone to your power. Bring them apart from their usual life, peers, families, and house. Give them the feeling of becoming oppressed, in limbo—they leave one world behind and join another. When alienated like this, they have little outside help, so they become easily deceived in their uncertainty.

Generate a Desire

People who have had some form of enjoyment in the past will try to replicate it or revisit it. The most deep-rooted and pleasurable experiences are typically from early childhood, which is sometimes unintentionally aligned with parental figures. Bring your victim back to that point by putting yourself in the triangle of the Oedipus and branding them as the needy kid. Unconscious of the reason for their emotional reaction they will be in love with you.

Prove yourself

Many people like to be seduced. If they oppose your efforts, it's certainly because you haven't gone that far to alleviate their suspicions — about your intentions, the intensity of your emotions, etc. A prompt intervention demonstrating how much you are able to go to prevail over them will dissipate the suspicions. Do not think about looking stupid or getting it wrong — any type of deed that is self-sacrificing will overwhelm your target's emotions, they will not realize anything else.

Mix the taboo and the transgression

Whatever one can do, there have always been cultural limits. A few of those, the most basic taboos, travel back decades; others are shallower, identifying appropriate polite behavior, for example. It's immensely seductive to make your victims feel that you are guiding them ahead of either type of boundaries. People are anxious to explore the dark side. If the impulse to violate attracts the victim to you, they would have trouble avoiding it. Bringing them further than they might imagine — the common sense of guilt and obligation generates a strong connection.

Pleasure and discomfort blend together

In seduction, the main error is being too sweet. Maybe your generosity is sweet at first, but it quickly becomes tedious; you're trying too much to please, so you seem nervous. Try to inflict some discomfort rather than overwhelming your victims with friendliness. Let them feel nervous and guilty. Incite a breakup — now a negotiated settlement, a switch to your previous kindness, will bring them down to their knees. The lower lows you build, the higher the ups. Creating the anticipation of terror to heighten the sexual effect.

Use the Lures of Spirit

Everyone seems to have suspicions and anxieties — of their own looks, self-worth, and gender identity. If your seduction caters solely to the looks, you will stir up those concerns and make your victims self-aware. Rather, by attempting to make them concentrate on something exquisite and spiritual, tempt them out of their anxieties: a spiritual experience, a noble piece of art, the occult. The target, lost in a divine mist, will feel refreshed, and carefree. Reinforce the impact of your seduction by attempting to make its sexual culmination appear as the two souls' true partnership.

Give them room to fall

If your victims get used to your aggression, they will offer less of their own energy and the pressure will slacken. You ought to get them up and switch the tables around. Pause for a moment when they are under your trap and they'll start coming after you. Give a hint that you're getting bored. Show interest in someone else. They would eventually try to literally control you and modesty would fly out of the window. Build the impression that they are seducing the seducer.

Chapter 9: How to Take Full Control of Your Relationship

Any sort of partnership has power dynamics at play. Then it should be no surprise that your loving relationship will also feature a power dynamic. There is a fair amount of control and reverence in some relationships and one party has more influence on others. The authority can shift at various points in your relationship to make things even more difficult. Maybe you both never spoke about control and reverence at the outset, so it was spread evenly. But then you found things changing as days progressed on and you started to feel like your wife or husband kind of had more authority.

9.1 Tips on Gaining Upper Hand in the Relationship

Hold on a second ... weren't you the couple's Beyoncé?

It's common in a relationship for the power balance to shift. There is a lot that could have changed the partnership structure. Yet if it's moved toward a different path (the one you do not adore), how can you stay on an equal playing field? If your guy got somewhat too "Kanye West" on you, how would you gain greater power and authority in the marriage? How can you turn this boat around and head into a safer, healthier

sea?

1. Speak.

Using your speech is one method to become more effective. Be transparent on your desires and your wishes. If you're not speaking up for yourself, who else would? Understand, he or she cannot read your thoughts. Then you must use the vocabulary to convince him/her everything you want and need in the relationship.

2. Have restrictions

Every person has their own list of norms and boundaries they're at ease with. You're going to have limits in your marriage and it's vital that you maintain them. For you, there are several things that will step over the line and you need to have the ability to draw that line strongly.

3. be more autonomous

Being independent and strong does not really mean you don't need your spouse in just about any way, it just means you, as a competent individual, you are able to do things yourself. It is crucial that you are able to be self-sufficient in a relationship. Your spouse will thank you and so will you for this sovereignty.

4. Stay true to your words

Saying stuff and doing the contrary is one way to ruin your respect very quickly. Actions tell a bigger picture —, particularly in relationships. Therefore, if you inform your partner that something will have certain consequences and you don't stay true to your words, he or she will not take you seriously. And even if you make a slight commitment to your partner, you have to honor the pledge.

5. The Golden rule

Rather than trying to follow the bricky yellow road, what if you follow the golden rule. A simple way to gain power is to treat your partner just the way you want to be treated. If you want consideration and respect, then you also need to give it to your partner as well.

6. Rest assured

If you're not respecting yourself, then why do you expect others to? It starts with you. You need to show how you want to be treated. This will be determined how you treat yourself. The manner in which you talk about yourself? Will you give some authority to yourself? What do you think of yourself? Take a minute to talk seriously about whether you regard yourself.

7. Don't just settle

For someone who understands what he or she deserves, there is nothing more comfortable and desirable. If you're in a partnership where your mate thinks he or she can get away with something, you have already lost respect and authority. Take a stand for yourself and don't care about walking away from a relationship that doesn't help you.

Chapter 10: Signs of Being Manipulated

Toxic individuals are exhausting, and physically wipe you down "They really need you to feel pity for them & to be accountable for all one's issues, and then they also want to solve these things.

The smartest gauge is to know that how you feel upon dealing with someone — our emotional and physical responses to individuals are our biggest drivers, noting that you must consider if you're more anxious, tense, or frustrated upon seeing this human, commuting with them, or speaking to them over the phone.

10.1 Dealing with a Toxic Person

Other indications to keep a watch out are if the individual is constantly condescending, compulsively in desire, and/or unwilling to take accountability or say sorry for one's behavior.

"It may be anyone who regularly takes narcotics or alcohol, lies, or wants you to lie about them, regulates or demeans what you've been doing. A toxic man's life is always personally, emotionally, financially, physically, and/or inter-personally out of balance.

Effect of Toxic People on Your Life

Toxic individuals can impact all aspects of people's lives and

we are always oblivious to that. We feel sympathy for them. The myths they inflict on us are accepted and rationalized. And this, in exchange, changes how we look about our values and ourselves. Toxic individuals are happy to drive happiness down from the stuff we previously enjoyed, such as jobs, relationships, interests, and even our self-love.

Setting Boundaries to Eliminate Manipulators

"If you feel unnoticed or misunderstood and feel manipulated or compelled to do stuff that is not even 'you' then you may be affected by a negative human. "Toxic individuals can make you question yourself or unconsciously do something that you wouldn't normally do—you might feel a need to be fit in or cool or get approval. Every situation is different but by influencing people to do something, toxic individuals may have a detrimental effect on others. They try to generate turmoil by negative behaviors: to use, to lie, to steal, to control, to criticize, to bully, to manipulate, to create conflict, and so on.

10.2 Signs of Being Manipulated

Most people do not realize whether they are being deceived until it's quite late. You know when you start to do, say, or believe things that serve them, you're being exploited as contrary to you. Good people inspire you to do the brightest and motivate you. Manipulators convince people that they

know what's best for you.

Then which are the warning signs – the real, clear indications if someone out there tries to manipulate us?

Blame Game

It does not matter how many times a toxic individual places you in painful scenarios on purpose, they are never going to excuse you for that. They are always finding reasons to keep you accountable for your acts.

Remember, for starters, the Xmas party where Sally the toxic person got wasted, made an embarrassment of herself and spoiled the entire night — then you blamed yourself for not controlling her alcohol consumption, suggesting that the whole thing was your fault?

Isolation

Did you notice you don't splurge time with friends and family anymore? A toxic friend will expect your undivided attention and make you feel guilty if they feel they don't give you enough of themselves.

For example, John a toxic person gets to control your entire time, to the large extent that he blurts out because he notices on social sites that you are trying to hang out with the other fellows and friends — that also without him. You realize then that you spend almost all of your leisure time with that kind of

individual and have completely overlooked how your other mates are like. This is not nice.

Always making you Guess about Them

One day they'll be absolutely delightful and then another day you'll wonder what you have done to get them upset. There is often nothing evident that will justify the shift in attitude-you know that there is something wrong. They may be prickly, cold, sad, cranky, or cold, and if you question them that there's something not right, the response is likely to be 'nothing' – but they'll just give you enough to make you realize that something is there. The 'just enough' could be a shuddering gasp, an eyebrow raised, a chilly shoulder. You may find yourself trying to make justifications for them when it happens or doing anything you could to keep them happy. See why that's working for them?

Quit trying to make them happy. Toxic people have long since figured out decent humans would go to exceptional measures to keep happy the individuals they value for. If your efforts to satisfy don't succeed, or if they don't last for long, then it's time to give up. Step back and return once the attitude has changed. You really aren't accountable for the emotions of someone else. If you really have executed anything to hurt someone unknowingly, ask, discuss this and apologize if need be. You don't have to conjecture at any cost.

Manipulative

If you feel like you are the only one that contributes to the friendship, you are probably correct. Poisonous people are capable of attempting to send out the feeling that it's something you are in debt for. Those people also have the means to take something from you or do things that upset you, and then maintain that they did it all for you. This is especially common in places of work or friendships in which power equilibrium is already out. Statements like these- 'I left you with that 6 months' value of filing. I thought you would praise the encounter and the chance to know your tasks for the filing containers.' Or, 'I'm hosting a dinner party. Why don't you bring a meal here? It will give you the opportunity to exhibit your kitchen expertise. You owe no-one any of it. If it is not feeling like a courtesy, it is not.

Do Not Own their Feelings

They will behave as if the emotions are yours, instead of possessing their own emotions. It is termed projection, as when they project their thoughts and feelings on you. For instance, you might have been accused of being upset with somebody who is frustrated but can't be held accountable for it. Could that be as dramatic as, "Are you all right with me? 'Or a little more straight forward, 'What's the reason for being mad at me,' or, 'why you have been down all day.' You're going to find yourself explaining and securing yourself and often that's going to happen constantly – because it has nothing to do with you. Be absolutely clear about what is about you and what is about them. If you feel like you are defending yourself far more times previously against baseless accusations or unfitting questions, you might be projected onto that one. You don't have to clarify, validate, or fight to protect yourself as well as cope with an allegation that was misfired. Bear that in mind.

Eggshells

Negative people prosper in trying to keep people on their toes and taking advantage of irrational tantrums. You never really know what kind of mood they're going to be in, so you're going to have to monitor what you're doing to them — or you're going to get 15 instant messages regarding a molehill of an issue that's resulted in a peak, including a lengthy list about all the excuses you're a bad guy, your life goes nowhere, and you are not as good enough as they are.

You may have a buddy such as Sean a toxic person who is unable to deal with an informal meetup. And there is a whole intense moment every time you see him, he brings up a problem you've caused or needed to fix, or necessitates you in an exhausting return that pressurizes you over and tends to make you doubt oneself and one's personality.

Makes you Prove Yourself to them

They will place you in a situation where you'll have to pick among them and some other thing on a regular basis – and you will always feel inclined to pick them. Poisonous people would wait till you have an involvement, therefore the drama would then emerge. 'If you ever really cared for me, you'd be skipping your exercise lesson and spending quality time with me.' The problem with this is that never enough is enough. Several events are deadly-unless its living or mortality, it's likely to be waiting.

Always trying to make you Feel Low

They're trying to pursue excuses why the interesting news is not perfect news. Examples are: For a promotion – 'Money is not so great for the type of work you are going to do.' For a vacation on the beach – 'Well weather will be hot. Do you think you would like to go? On becoming a Universe Queen– 'Well you know the Universe isn't that big, and I am sure that you're not going to have breaks.' don't let someone discourage you or reduce you to their own size. You do not need their authorization anyway – and for that issue anybody else's.

Never Says Sorry

Before they really make an apology they would then hide the truth, so there is no reason to argue. They're going to spin the words, alter the way it occurred and so persuasively re-enact it they're going to believe their own baloney. People don't have to excuse themselves to be incorrect. And you do not need to go ahead with an apology. Just go on-without others. Don't give up your facts but don't carry on with the reasoning. There is really no point here. Some individuals would like to be correct more than they'd like to be delighted and you have got better stuff to do than providing the right-combatants with fodder.

No Closure on the Issue

They are not going to pick up your phone. They will not respond to messages and emails. and among the sessions of their voice mail, you may discover oneself attempting to play the discussion or reasoning in your head again and again and again, speculating about personal life, wondering what you've done to hurt them, or if they're deceased, lively, or even just neglecting you – which can all experience this at key moments. People caring for you are not going to let you feel total crap without going to figure it out. It doesn't imply obviously that you are going to sort it out, but still, at a minimum, they're going to try. If they end up leaving you 'out there' for long sessions, take that as a signal of people's assets within the interaction.

Irrelevant Things while Conversing

When you are attempting to solve things that are essential to

you, harmful people come up with insignificant stuff from five justifications before. The issue with it is that you are attempting to argue on something you appears to have done 6 months ago prior to you understand it, also defending yourself instead of dealing with the problem. Not only, has it just seemed too often end up with what you did to them.

Toxic tone- non-toxic words

The tone may be ignorant enough and much more is conveyed in the tone. Things like, "what have you been doing today? 'Can mean something different regarding how it's said. It might mean something from 'I think you have done nothing - as normal' to 'I'm certain your day went great than mine. Mine was horrific. Just horrifying. And you haven't even noticed enough to ask.' When you ask the tone, they're going to be back with, 'What I said was what you did today,' which is true, but not really.

Altering the main focus while conversing

You may be trying to fix the problem or get clarity, and before you know it, the conversation/reasoning has relocated away from the topic which was essential to you and then onto the way you talked about – whether there is a problem with your way of doing it or not. You'll see yourself justifying your attitude, your movements, your word usage, or the manner you move your belly while you take a breath – it doesn't really

have to make any sense. Your original desire, whereas, has gone well on the heap of unresolved discussions that continue to get larger day by day.

Exaggeration.

'You never ...' you always' ...' It's impossible to protect yourself from this abuse. Poisonous people have a habit of trying to draw on the yet another time you did not or the one you did as proof of your inadequacies. Don't let yourself into the reasoning. You are not going to win. And then you just don't have to.

Judgmental.

Quite often we all have it wrong and people who are harmful would then make it sure that you have got it. They are going to demean you and point a finger at self-esteem that suggests you are much less since you made an error. We are all permitted to have it mistaken now and then but no one has the courage to stand in judgment unless we've conducted something which impacts them.

Chapter 11: How to Win Friends with Persuasion?

To me, it is not for beauty to be "appealing." It's about the whole vibe of a person — are they fascinating and interested, are they making me chuckle, do they appear kind? And a huge part of figuring this out initially gets down to what other person is communicating via body language.

Now I'm not saying that you can figure out everything else about yet another individual just by how they do it or by not tilting their heads. All I'm saying is that accessible and welcoming body language creates a big difference when it comes to how relaxed I feel when I get to know someone that creates it far simpler to find out the important bits, like whether we have common beliefs, or not.

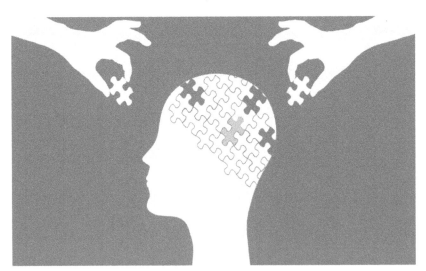

11.1 Techniques to Win Friends

Smile (But Not Right Away)

Have you really observed that somehow smiles are highly contagious? When you smile it's hard to not smile back for others. Well, now, science supports that assumption.

When people glance at an image of someone else happy, they find it incredibly hard to frown. It's just too easy to return a smile that conducting something else takes concentrated effort.

One of the greatest things you can do anytime you walk into a room is to place a sincere smile across your lips. In return, you'll build a successful chain reaction that will take you throughout the day.

Smiling influences the way we perceive the feelings of others from another report by analysing the electrical impulses in the brains of volunteers, the team has found that smiling makes we view the individuals around us as more optimistic.

They found, specifically, that when people don't smile, they interpret "neutral" faces as "neutral." even so, once people smile, they misinterpret "neutral" facial expressions as "glad."

So the world has become a happier place when people smile. Do you think that looking more optimistic at the folks around you would start making you quite common to speak to them?

It's really not a secret we love being around happy people. We feel comfortable when we see somebody with a sincere smile or happiness on their lips. We also naturally see individuals smile as relaxed, which is a very attractive characteristic.

Did you realize that your brain produces healthy chemicals while you smile which can help boost your mood? With more dopamine running into the bloodstream, you will feel better for yourself and have a higher likelihood of helping others.

Smiling is effective amongst many others. If we smile more often, then we want to talk to others as well. The more individuals we speak to, the more relaxed we are. The more assured we feel, the far more organic it becomes to smile.

Then, why not check it out. Be all smiles at the pedestrians on the road you walk. Smile into the mirror to oneself. Watch each morning just a few mins of comedy. To smile often, do anything it requires. Your body and brain will thank you.

Use Eye Contact to Create Better Relationships

Do you ever question why many individuals seem so quick to find new friends when others consider it hard to establish productive new relationships?

It's the appropriate use of eye contact in several cases that makes the distinction!

Researchers have found how one of the most significant

differences among people who are relatively self - assured and who make more friends, and those who are quiet and reserved would be that self-assured people make eye contact with their listeners far more often.

There are many introverted people that avoid eye contact when they talk to someone. They prefer to glance away or downwards rather than glancing at the individual they're referring to.

If you've been far less popular in trying to make buddies than you really want, by trying to make this one easy shift in your conduct, you might become ready to be more social and outgoing.

Do Not Criticize, Condemn, or Complain

Any fool, yet most fools can condemn critique or whine. For being forgiving requires self-control and character, this practice would then give major dividends throughout the relationships with other people.

Eye Contact

Learn how to efficiently use eye contact while you are trying to talk to someone. Some of us rarely allow eye contact while we are interacting with our discussion companion. This can make others think of us as anxious and dishonest. Many of them, on the other side, make much more eye contact and look too

deeply. This also renders our partners in conversations uneasy. Follow the correct balance of eye contact as well as gaze away. Most of North Americans, particularly the Caucasians, chose to get a great deal with eye contact while talking to somebody. When a person fails to build eye contact with them, they tend to think something is fishy about that person. The mere term "shifty-eyed" denotes an individual whose eyes move about the room, which means they are unreliable. When talking to someone who's from either a cultural value that chooses a great deal of eye contact, be careful to keep trying to look at that individual regularly while speaking, even as you think what to say after that. A penetrating gaze you don't have to use, a pleasant stillness will do. If it always upsets you to stare straight at the eyes of another human, you should gaze at the expression of another human without relying entirely on the eyes.

When you usually point at the region of the ear or the nasal bridge that is near enough to get to the center of the head to glance into that person's eyes.

You can think it's calming your own anxiety by having your view go somewhat out of sight. If you are talking to others, hold the attention on the other person for the most part. If you look too much around the room or look at other people too often, your friend may assume you're annoyed, or you're

looking for somebody else you'd prefer to talk to. If you have trouble knowing precisely how to start making eye contact, you could even receive support from exercising before a mirror, or with someone else.

But don't stare too intensely at others!

A very intensified, gaze start could even make your partner being very uneasy with the conversation. To be on the other end of an extreme glare, especially at close distance, can be quite uncomfortable. You can lighten your impression by smiling more frequently, nodding, and gazing at the whole face and also the eyes. You may also regularly look away for short periods. Try staring at the expression of your discussion partner when you talk, and add in plenty of smiles and gestures, sometimes turning away as you chat and listen. It will demonstrate you are polite, involved, and open. If other people have the perception that you really actually listen to them and happily talk to them, they'll be far more probable to choose to have more discussions with you.

11.2 Protect Others' Pride and Win Big

While success may seem to come by uplifting yourself over others, in fact, the perfect way to succeed is to establish a sincere interest in others. Defending the dignity of others through trying to avoid criticisms and clashes is the very first

move to win them over and persuade the others to listen to your viewpoint.

You should really be courteous, applauding your listeners instead of critiquing them as a basic guideline, in order to build someone else up as well as change their views. Everyone believes one's own name is the "loveliest voice" they've ever listened to, so a true leader believes first of all on how to uplift others around him. Analyze and make gentle, kind suggestions, instead of challenging or directing the people with whom you lead or collaborate. By trying to make others believe that your own great, honorable concepts are in fact their own, you are far more likely to build trusting relationships than if you are continuously disagreeing or trying to show superiority.

Likewise, accept your own errors, and accept them. It might seem intuitive to the contrary as empowerment is frequently represented as somehow about superiority and demonstrating your toughness. But ignoring responsibility and trying to downplay your own mistakes while pointing out others is in fact an indication of vulnerability. If you are honest and open about your imperfections you will become more convincing.

Listen More, Talk Less

How to succeed in making buddies and influence other people is at its core regarding communicating effectively. But rather than mastering the art of trying to argue and propaganda,

carefully establish the skill of good listener. When you approach people with open-mindedness and friendly attitude, they are much more inclined to share as well as collaborate with you than to try and compete with you.

Listening to someone, we know so much about them: for starters, their goals, aspirations, expectations, value structures, beliefs, and perspectives. Realizing what helps make someone else tick is the very first move to convince them and lead them.

An attitude of silent but effective listening is better, rather than trying to control every discussion. Motivate individuals around you to speak about yourself and their priorities and you will be much more likable. And when you're talking, you must talk more about your discussion partner's interests and less concerning yourself. Whenever it comes to persuasive, charismatic dialogue, smaller is better. Talking is cheap but able to listen is absolutely priceless. Remembering the name of a person, having to ask individuals questions to motivate them to speak for themselves so that you can find their passions and interests is what makes us believe that you really like them, and they like you in turn. In two months you start making more friends by becoming honestly interested in people than you could ever in 2 years by attempting to get some other individuals taking an interest in you." If you strip it down, you must hear to 75% and speak only 25% of the time.

Know the Value of Charm

One thing people don't talk a lot about in the job hunting sector is that much of having the chance isn't really about skill, in which university you went to university and whom you recognize, its people who like you. A decent cv that brings you through the door, but charisma, social abilities, and potential can hold you there because people would usually pick the person they enjoy staying around over an applicant they wouldn't appreciate staying around very much but are much more skilled. Become someone like people would want to talk to, be truly curious about people because that will enhance your living and create many more options than you ever imagined possible.

Be Quick To Acknowledge Your Own Mistakes

Nothing can make you less hostile and more friendly if you are patient enough and fair enough to accept your inner weaknesses. Having good and healthy professional and personal relations depends on you, particularly your shortcomings, taking full accountability of your acts. Nothing would help ease the stress or conflict on your part more than a simple acceptance and apologizing.

Chapter 12: Watch the Behaviour of People

Everybody is distinctive; everybody has different behaviors. What would be more enjoyable than in a café, resting in a park on a bench, or on a terrace, watching other people pass by? Movements, gestures, verbal and nonverbal behavior-you will track anything.

It's interesting to watch people, see their behaviors, and look at their productivity, for many reasons. It's enjoyable but it's very interesting as well. Realizing what inspires people, why they do what they do, and how they respond to the impacts around them would only lead to life quality enhancements.

12.1 People Observation

We called this "people observation" technique because it explains effectively what it actually is. Some of you might think that the language of the body is this.

Perfecting the Body Language: how to notice People's Mind Non verbally

Of course, the purpose of body language is to track and interpret the gestures, but the interpretation of people is not restricted to only that.

Observation of persons builds from the following measures:

Body moves

Expressions on face

Language-Conduct

Way of Thought

Political views

Correlations regarding the above

Observation of the People: why and how to do it

Let's say you haven't been so social in the past. You had recognized your issue and was wondering what your choice would be to change that.

You always needed a number of friends. Rather you might be more defined as boring. So for me to become more enjoyable and unexpected you had to modify your own attitudes.

First, you began reading regarding body language and habits of action which can show what people think. You got to learn many trends and tried to recognize them in others each time you would go out.

One's greatest challenge would be forcing your eyes wide open each time. You see, it was a little difficult to hold your concentration on other people's gestures, particularly at the start.

You must be cautious to not get too centered while monitoring someone else because you're going to give a weird person's impression. Also, to make associations among their motions and their phrases you must notice what the other people have been saying.

There are two important components of body language. The main body movement (legs, hands, posture, etc.) as well as the expressions.

You could only identify basic moves at the start of the observation. When you were with someone who had performed a specific pattern at a given time, try to confirm their feelings and thoughts at that time the next moment.

You only needed to make sure their actions were relevant compared to what you had been researching. Of course, you did not question people what they felt directly; merely informal questions...

As you are outside keep watching the men. Reach a level at which you could concentrate on your observation at the same time and give full focus to everything else the person told.

Finally, understand that this technique had become a talent stored in the memory system of the procedures. As you practice the technique, you would then understand the process and your subconscious will be able to understand the response of other people even if your focus is not aimed at the strategy.

That's great because you'll have a perpetual instinctive reflex regarding the persons you encounter that will always be right. In conversations with others, you should have an edge and connect easier.

Now we'll see the stages of the technique as well as how the method can be implemented in your daily life.

The "Observation of the People" technique

Expressions

That's the second most popular type of body dialect. Seek to grasp the features of the hands. It can offer you far more info about other people's inner world. Yet they too are more difficult to spot.

One must confess that it really is challenging to understand trends in facial expressions. Initially begin with the fundamentals using the same techniques as the body gestures.

You will finally be able to detect various expressions. You have to take the very same measures as you appear to have done with the phase of the movements.

If you achieve a point at that you can interpret other people's body language then you can know how much you have improved your curiosity towards others. This expertise will give a competitive advantage when you interact with others.

A helpful tip to help you understand the language of your body better is to examine one's body movements and sentiments, and how the two to correlate.

This could be your initial body language practice; to interpret your body while communicating with others.

Body moves

Base your attention on many acts, as described earlier. The very first 2 are body language sections.

You have to identify some specific body language moves. Purchasing a good book associated with it will be doing the tactic.

First, learn the main body's movements, so they are easy to identify. That would be an easy starting point. Each time you are outside, strive to remember similar behavior.

Gold is what patience is. There's no purpose in reading the entire book in a week and intending to immediately

implement its strategies. That is clearly not feasible.

Note, this is really a process and it involves time and practice for the mind to learn and consciously or unconsciously utilize it. Trust your instincts, then.

Slowly you will be identifying identical patterns every day in different individuals. This situation will cause the linkages between the movement patterns and the feelings in their mind.

When you feel that all the directed movements can be detected easily, continue towards the other one. This is a good way to enhance all body motions and eventually, you'll also be capable of detecting numerous motions and clusters of movement.

The hint is to be patient. It is a People Observation requirement.

Language

Let's use psychology now. Observation of certain people's language and attitudes will give you useful knowledge regarding their personality style.

Notice when they talk to those who use a lot of "me" or "I." That shows a likely focus on one's ego. And also glance for "defensive" expressions because a "defending" behavior may result from the accentuated ego.

People with poor self-esteem are seeking to conceal their actual selves. You can spot them by the dialect they are using.

In a fictional scenario, they usually exaggerate and stress how they might react. The reality of course is distinct in several cases.

Observing the words people are using, you will tell that they are healthy, evil, emotional, or just if they have psychological problems or a traumatic childhood background.

You have to relate all those characteristics to the language they use.

12.2 Watching the Behavior

Have you really sat and watched in a restaurant that has different people tables? It will not only be fascinating people observing, it may even be analysed into human patterns. Will an individual at one table control the discussion, raising their arms in violent hand motions while another participant sits mutely, listening to and absorbing what other person is saying? Do people at a different table appear to be drenched in a conversation that might cross on an assertion? What does all of this mean?

It is important to consider the various behavioral styles first, in order to better understand the complexities in play. Most individuals are on a lifetime search for one of the following things: outcomes, communication, reliability, or factual information, and this search influences how they most of the time behave. This doesn't imply someone who is pushed by results also doesn't appreciate interconnection or reliability; it just means that people often have one style of behavior and attitude which appears to be more dominant than others. Public observation of these styles can give you a pretty good idea of how particular persons are connected and how they act the way they do.

Real-world experience in a restaurant

Identifying a few of the cognitive patterns in effect can be relatively easy at a normal restaurant. The immersive individual will ask them their name when the server first welcomes them, want to know a little bit about them as well find out for how long they've been working here. They will connect with the server. They tend to talk quickly with plenty of gestures and always, first and primarily, consider the individual they are communicating to. While they're going to interact a lot and lead the discussion, they're going to be mindful of having the other individual in mind, preventing any contact that's too overt.

This is the doers that are motivated by performance. They directly communicate, are fast-paced as well as appear to have been task-oriented. Those people would typically be there on the phone pre or post buying their meals, emailing, or text attempting to increase their performance. Chances are, instead of full sentences, the messages will be given with simple sentences or bullet points because results-oriented individuals would like stuff done now. They'll definitely know just whatever they like to consume before the waitress comes to the table so they'll be eager about placing the order.

The calm person is going to be respectful and comfortable, not hasty. They're going to make the waiter chat about food offerings, regular sales and they're going to have some informal talking. Not wanting to offend the server, that much if they know it already what they will be ordering, the consistent individual might ask the server's opinion on a meal. Communication could even start with phrases like "if you don't bother," "if it isn't too enough distress," or "I absolutely despise disrupting" with others at the table in an attempt to lighten the straightforwardness. The seekers for stabilization and doing anything in one's control not to toe the line. They are stagnant directed than in the first 2 categories but they target the people like the engaging group. if this had been a sports betting table rather than a cafe, those will be the individuals to witness even though they prefer to keep one's emotions under control and typically show one's devilish smile.

The individual based on facts seems to be task-oriented as well as operates at a moderate speed, involved with knowing the appropriate details before continuing. This person should be one of those at the table to question what components are in any meal, side dish and sauce and how they could be replaced, changed, or omitted or not. They are trying to ask why a certain seasoning is being used with a certain meal and, oddly enough, they are going to be the last person to order at the table, taking their chance to create their ideal decision. Since these decisive conversationalists are far less worried about inconveniencing someone than to be wrong, those who will pose questions till they feel at ease that they have all the details they need to resolve a scenario, even if it is merely placing an order.

The discussion will probably be fascinating with those 4 personality types sitting at a table. The participatory person will significantly contribute the discussion obviously but would then do so ideologically in an attempt to earn acquaintances. The facts and results will be more straightforward and will be the candidate most likely to say stuff that could be considered rude either to the participatory or reliable person. The outcomes individual may analyze a great thing they have during a discussion and the conspiracy theories-based individual will ask several more "why" queries to effectively understand the subject of the discussion. The queries may get annoying for the result-oriented individual who really doesn't wish to have to clarify their self in this

detail.

The steady speaker will place everyone else first and notice their social skills, doing their finest at the table to listen to it and comprehend the other viewpoints. The person guided by the results would be the first one to look at their watch, curious to know when the meal will eventually be presented.

Tolerance is not a core value for the person guided by the outcomes. The participatory individual would have to contend with the desire to control the discussion. By now, the person on the basis of facts has calculated their meal's calorie count yet to show up.

Mannerisms

The results-driven people's body language is easy to identify: standing hand in pocket, going to lean forward, walking briskly and speaking with tons and tons of the over-emphasized hand movements. Now, those who want the details and the very first time they would like to listen to it right. The participatory person tries to switch his weight a lot and in a discussion, his hands seem to be everywhere. This person will most likely bump into someone or something when strolling, and they're too busy to look at all the individuals around. Expect plenty of large movements and facial expressions from such jovial people while having a conversation.

Body language signs for the stable person involve slouching with the hand in the pocket, strolling at such a comfortable, constant speed, and the infrequent gesture all through discussion. For the reality-driven person, body language indications include having to stand with their arms rolled up onto their chin with one hand whilst they process the information. They walk in a specific horizontal path and when interacting they have next to no hand gestures, rather opting to stay very restrained as they soak up the details around them.

12.3 Conflicts between different types of behavior

The individual who enjoys to actually debate larger picture notions can quickly become irritated by the person asking a lot of follow-up questions (generally the fact grabber), needing a much more clear analysis of how everything is in the manner it is. Fact seekers will ask lots of questions and feel stress unless they fully answer the questions to their satisfaction. Likewise, based on their pace, the slow and gradual individual may well be placed off (and conversely) by the outcomes thoughtful person. The person who results wants answers right now, and when it feels right, the stable individual gets around to the catchphrase. The intensity of each person will generate unease for other individuals.

When it comes to discussion two participatory individuals at the very same table will start competing for superiority. Like two dogs struggling for alpha dog position, the other persons involved, such as the server, would find it challenging to get a word in mid-sentence.

The individual who is high in solidity would generally get along well with somebody who is social since they respect people and appreciate them. And it produces a complementary dynamic because the engaging individual likes to chat and when the urge hits, the calm person is fully satisfied tossing into a thought.

The person focused on the evidence would possibly also get on well with a stable individual well. The steady person does not need to pose a ton of queries; they become difficult to comprehend. The truths-based individual will directly communicate, while the calm person will try to smooth the discussion with comments that render the contactless straightforward. Possibilities are, both, just like social and calm individuals, would be complimentary too.

Chapter 13: How to Get Rid Of Manipulative People?

Some people in this world only exist and flourish because they are constantly using someone to their benefit in order to get ahead. Manipulators have the capacity to make someone else feel as if they've been supposed to pay something, but often pounce on hard-working, unselfish people who are more likely to be manipulated in their job. If you're in a situation where somebody is attempting to sway you, notice: You all are your own individual. Don't let anyone leave you feeling any differently.

13.1 Techniques

Addressing the Issue

The very first strategy for dealing with a devious person is to realize that you're being exploited, either in a job or in your private life. Such people will consider you to drift everything that you do when they need help and are extremely overwhelming in their requirements for help. They don't see your requirements in the least bit while they require you to do something, and they see their requirements as the highest concern. If you realize co-workers or so-called mates putting their own needs ahead of yours, then immediately start to take measures to sabotage their efforts.

Inquire

Manipulators will try to even get you to do things with hardly any questions raised for them. So when you ask them a question it changes the power balance to your side so very marginally. Ask them how or why a quest would help all interested participants, or whether they really believe it is fair what they are looking for. If they are honest they will have to admit they are a little irrational or nonsensical. If they choose not to be truthful, you've shifted control even further to your own side, as there's no justification to do something for someone who is less than true to you.

Retain Strong

In older person clothing manipulators just are pricks. They are preying on those they feel would not speak-up for themselves and they think they will still get whatever they want. Manipulators, however, lose power completely once their perpetrator is standing up for their rights before them. They're so used to getting their bidding accomplished for them that they also have no clue what to do if someone disregards their requirements. They will often try and influence your decision by standing firm against such a manipulator. Don't let them do it. Only you can control yourself; compromising just once can lead to a slippery slope where aggressors are constantly victimizing you.

Use your time to benefit

Manipulators start making demands as well as enforce time limits which cause major pressure to their perpetrators. But it's your time. If someone you know tries to take benefit of you, demands that you complete the task over a certain amount of time, inform them that you will "think about it." Doing so is as useful as completely tearing them down. In reality, going to string them along turns the table on the deceiver entirely, because they would be the ones looking for you to learn. Of course, you do not want to be the manipulator, but allowing the aggressor a dose of their very own medicine can't harm your own purpose.

Set repercussions

The demands that manipulators enforce on others who are mandates which must be fulfilled in their eyes. They're going to be doing their utmost to make it feel that you owe something to them, and have to do what they're doing. In fact, it's they who might owe you when you do such individuals this massive favor. Make that absolutely clear to those people. This works particularly if you do have other regulations that need your urgent attention. If they find that they are going to end up getting to do something in exchange for you, they would more than likely retract their demand. Although they will possibly try and find another target instead of actually

finishing the work on their own, you have at least managed to get them off you.

Conclusion

Dark psychology is a concept of human cognition and an analysis of the human experience as it refers to the psychological essence of people to prey on others driven by psychopathic, psychopathological or deviant criminal impulses that transcend intent and basic principles in instinctual forces, scientific theory, and evolutionary biology. Most of mankind has an ability to victimize many living beings and humans. Although a number of people suppress or sublimate this urge, certain people regularly execute such urges. Dark psychology investigates the personalities of deviants, terrorists, and people doing cybercrimes. Dark psychology is the capacity of manipulating the emotions of people. We also have this power and consciously and unknowingly make use of it too. This is a mental game where we compete with the emotions, desires, experiences, etc. of certain individuals in order to fulfill oneself by attaining desirable goals. We can say, for example, that a salesman is very genuinely enthusiastic about selling his products to the client while using dark psychology to influence the clients. He is deliberately doing so. On the other side, an egoistic person plays the game of one's subconscious to unknowingly satisfy the needs of others. Dark psychology which occurs unknowingly can be quite dangerous as it can deeply affect the feelings of others. It's not healthy to deliberately refer to someone, too.

Manipulation of darkness is an incredible weapon that can control darkness or mist. That is the reverse of the Manipulation of Light. This superpower's users can build, form, and control the shadow or darkness for different degrees of results, shapes, sizes, and intensities. Based on the degree of energy, one can easily use this amazing force to shroud an entire region, nation, or even this planet in everlasting darkness for the whole time. Besides that, this capacity is as productive as one wishes and relies on the consumer for its control.

We are knowingly seeing dark psychological strategies in our daily lives. The manipulators secretly strike us and we couldn't even know it. Manipulators use techniques in that matter, consciously. Some secret manipulators deliberately say and do stuff for influence and leverage to have what they want to get.

The methods of coercion include implicit violence, narcissistic bullying, criticism, and indirect kinds of emotional harassment. These are the guns that are commonly used:

Having the remorse and the embarrassment sound

Comparing you against another

To deceive and refute

What you favor

Complaining about you

Should not think

Emotional blackmail

Showing sympathy

Playing around in your subconscious

To apologize

Those techniques are used for awareness by manipulators. These toxic tricks can be traumatic to you, and can also harm your self-worth. We will figure out how to negotiate with selfish and challenging people for our own self-protection.

There are good and bad aspects of any single event in this universe. If we can use dark psychology to influence the minds of people for the betterment of human civilization, that's going to be great. There are too many sinister psychological strategies for someone to exploit. We can use these techniques with ease and of course knowledge. We have to remember that while using tricks, not to be the reason for any kind of harm to others.

Below are a few tactical strategies and suggestions for controlling the minds of the people. Let's use them for craft:

Smile While Speaking: It will make people feel relaxed with you and open up to you.

Eye contact: This helps to make you sharp and smart in front of others. People are going to be treating you and your expressions seriously.

Being nice to others: Say "hello" to your neighbors as well as others you know and maintain yourself as a well-behaved person before them

Making people happy: When you intend to manipulate someone's mind you will be able to make them happy because laughing makes them comfortable.

Keep quiet: If you don't ask for more information, keep silent then the other individual will automatically fill your thirst. On the other side, if you decide to resist others while being quiet, he/she will quit bothering you.

Help others feel comfortable around you: Say the names of others with love when communicating. Do not ever make a circumstance humiliating. Give them an opportunity to try to understand.

Start arguing: Don't really attempt to reason because you realize he/she is thinking anything, don't mention anything outright. Let them stop and try using constructive terms to get them to realize the truth.

Handling a hostile person: Stay silent and only use the very thing that would explicitly assault him/her. That way he/she is going to be monitored.

So the deep ideology and deception can function like this.